Acting for Animators

A Complete Guide to Performance Animation

Ed Hooks

Foreword by Brad Bird

Illustrations by Mike Caputo

HEINEMANN
Portsmouth, NH

Heinemann
A division of Reed Elsevier Inc.
361 Hanover Street
Portsmouth, NH 03801–3912
www.heinemanndrama.com

Offices and agents throughout the world

Library of Congress Cataloging-in-Publication Data
Hooks, Ed.
    Acting for animators : a complete guide to performance animation / Ed Hooks ;
    foreword by Brad Bird ; illustrations by Mike Caputo.
        p.   cm.
    Includes bibliographic references.
    ISBN 0-325-00229-0 (paperback)
     1. Animation (Cinematography). 2. Motion picture acting. I. Title.

TR897.5. H66 2000
791.43'7—dc21   00-040961

Editor: Lisa A. Barnett
Production: Vicki Kasabian
Electronic product developers: Dan Breslin and Eyeon Interactive
Cover and text illustrations: Mike Caputo
Cover design: Michael Leary/Michael Leary Design
Manufacturing: Deanna Richardson

Printed in the United States of America on acid-free paper
04   03   02   01   VP   2   3   4   5

For Ken Bielenberg, who first asked me, "Would you be willing to teach acting on-site? I work for an animation company."

Indeed, the more the arts develop the more they depend on each other for definition.

— E. M. Forster, Aspects of the Novel

Contents

Foreword by Brad Bird   vi

Acknowledgments   viii

Introduction   1

1   Seven Essential Acting Concepts   7

2   The Audience   19

3   Character   25

4   The Scene   40

5   Movement and Body Language   61

6   Speech   79

7   The Camera   83

8   Technique   87

9   The Form   96

10   The Medium   101

11   Classroom Exercises   106

12   The Iron Giant: An Acting Analysis   110

Postscript: What Is Method Acting?   118

Recommended Reading and Other Resources   120

Works Cited   122

Foreword

One never hears about how many tubes of paint Picasso used to create *Guernica*, the exact number of notes contained in Gershwin's "Rhapsody in Blue," or how many facial expressions Brando deployed in *On the Waterfront*.

Yet when the art of character animation is discussed at all, it is usually in mind-numbingly numeric terms, with statements along the lines of "more than 23 skadrillion drawings were used in the production of *Rumpelstiltskin*. If each drawing were laid end to end, they would reach to Jupiter and back 6.7 times."

When an art form is so consistently described in such a dreary way it's easy to see why animation is often thought to be more technique than art, and its practitioners little more than technicians with pencils (or clay or pixels or puppets) in the eyes of the public.

When an animated character breaks through and becomes part of the cultural land-scape, the voice actor—not the animator—is credited, because people understand what a voice actor does.

A friend of mine supervised the animation of a lead character in a major animated feature. In many interviews the well-known actress who voiced the character immod-estly claimed that the animators had simply, in effect, copied her mannerisms and per-formance. In reality the animators had found her acting style generic and boring, and had turned elsewhere for inspiration: to people they had known in their own lives, friends and members of their families, even to studying Julia Louis Dreyfuss in episodes of *Seinfeld*.

What is typically lost in discussions about animation is the fact that when you watch an animated film, the performance you're seeing is the one *the animator* is giving to you. If an animated character makes you laugh or cry, feel fear, anger, empathy, or a million other emotions, it is largely due to the work of these often unsung artists, who invest a lot of themselves in the creation of these indelible moments.

If the public could watch the faces of the best animators when caught up in the act of drawing an emotional scene, they would see artists as fully invested *in the moment* as the best live actors. The difference is that an animator *stays* in that moment, often working for weeks to express an emotion his or her character takes only seconds to convey onscreen. The art of character animation, then, is to try to catch lightning in a bottle one volt at a time.

Countless books have been dedicated to the graphics, the look, the techniques, the *process* of character animation, but precious little has been written about performance, which is nothing less than the heart of the matter. As with any art, the vast majority of animation is garbage. It overflows with "characters"—human and not, male, female, fat, thin, tall, short, young, old, and in-between; characters who possess different voices, different clothes, head shapes, skin color, hair color, characters that have in fact only one thing in common—they all move exactly alike.

Ed Hooks knows that in the very best animated films, movement defines character: Lady moves differently than Tramp, Woody moves differently than Buzz, and Wallace moves nothing like Gromit. By looking outside the medium itself, and by intelligently and thoughtfully examining character animation from an actor's perspective, Mr. Hooks has made a valuable contribution toward deepening our understanding of it.

I have no idea how many hours it took Mr. Hooks to write this book, how many gallons of ink was used in its printing, or how far it would stretch if you laid each copy of this edition end to end.

And I hope to God it never comes up.

Brad Bird

Acknowledgments

I would like to thank the many people who helped, inspired, and prodded me toward the completion of this book: Doug Aberle, Robin Ator, Heather Annseley, Jo McGinley, Sven Pannicke, Brad Blackbourn, Angie Jones, Mike Caputo, Alberto Menache, Larry Bafia, Jean Newlove, Leslie Bishko, and Patrick Kenny.

Special thanks to Rick May, who runs CG-CHAR, the absolute best listserv for animators on the Internet. And, of course, mega-thanks to all of the animators on the listserv who have been patient with my questions about their art form and who were willing to debate and discuss many of the acting principles set forth in this book. I continue to learn much from you, and I'm deeply grateful.

I'd also like to thank Lisa Barnett, my editor at Heinemann, as well as Vicki Kasabian and Dan Breslin, who coordinated this project's book and CD production.

Thanks to Claudia, Paolo, and the staff at Torrefazione Italia on University Avenue in Palo Alto, California, a wonderful Italian coffee house that frequently doubles as my office. That's me sitting in the window with my laptop.

My wife, Cally, and especially my daughter, Dagny, are to be applauded: it's difficult to understand why Dad has to spend so much time writing and complaining about deadlines, and I appreciate your patience.

And thanks to those—past and present—who have inspired me: John Canemaker, Frank Thomas and Ollie Johnston, Don Graham, Walt Disney, Michael Barrier, Konstantin Stanislavsky, Michael Chekhov, and my acting students.

Introduction

My first class with animators took place in April 1996, at Pacific Data Images in Palo Alto, California. PDI hired me to teach acting to some of their character animators on-site when the company went into preproduction for its first feature film, *Antz*. I had been teaching professional-level acting classes for more than twenty years, but this was my first exposure to the world of animation. Oh sure, I was a fan like everybody else. I could tell you the plot points of the famous Disney films and was still traumatized by the shooting death of Bambi's mother, but the actual process of animation was a total mystery to me. I had never heard of *squash and stretch*, *in-betweening*, or *pose to pose*. To me, 3-D was a blast from the past involving cheap white-and-green plastic glasses and headache-evoking out-of-focus images on a movie screen. I had not yet seen the first successful computer-generated (CG) feature film, *Toy Story*, and I thought the whole catalogue of computer animation know-how was contained in the games my daughter played on the living room television set.

In short, I had no way of knowing as I stood before that group in PDI's sunny activities room that I was embarking on a grand adventure into what is probably *the* major art form of the twenty-first century. I didn't know that animation would kick me creatively in the same way acting did twenty-five years earlier as a new acting student in New York. I didn't realize that, in a few short years, animation would take me all around the world, introduce me to extraordinarily talented people, and expose me to achievements in art that border on the magical. I had no way of knowing that my life was about to change.

After some clumsy and humorous fits and starts during which I handed out scenes from stage plays and tried to teach acting to the PDI animators the way one would teach it to actors, our classes settled into a weekly pattern of (1) a lecture on acting theory, (2) improvisational exercises, and (3) screening clips from live-action movies to illustrate acting principles. This book is an extension of that beginning. Since 1996, I've made it my business to be an attentive student of animation, and I think I've learned a lot about what animators do. I finally know what squash-and-stretch means, for starters, and I realize that animators approach acting from a different perspective than actors do. The primary distinction is that actors want to get up on the stage and strut their stuff, while animators want their *characters* to get up on stage. Actors create emotion—largely internally—in the present moment, while animators *describe* internal emotion through the external movement of their characters. Animators are oriented to what actors disparagingly call "results." From a trained actor's perspective, the way animators come at the subject is upside down. An animator is concerned with whether a character's eyebrows should be raised to show curiosity, how many blinks occur in an excited moment, whether it is the head or the shoulders that first turn for a sideways glance, how to indicate emotion. Actors, by contrast, think about such things rarely, if ever, because they are taught *not* to play results. Emotions and facial expressions are results of inner motivation. An actor strives to find intention and motivation, which manifests itself in the actions he plays and objectives he pursues. He is taught that whatever emotion and facial/body movement are appropriate to the moment will just naturally happen. If an actor-in-training asked his teacher if he should lift his eyebrows to suggest curiosity, the teacher would likely be dumbfounded. Actors shouldn't be thinking about eyebrows!

This book will not teach you how to draw or manipulate pixels on a screen. I'm starting with the premise that my reader either already knows those skills or is currently being instructed by experienced animators. I begin with *how* to bring life to those characters you're creating. The goal of this book is to interpret and filter the basic principles of acting so that you can apply them to animation. In your work as an animator, you need to know a lot about acting, but you don't need to know everything about it. You don't, for example, need to learn how to make yourself cry because, if you were to do that, you wouldn't be able to see to animate.

But I'm getting ahead of myself. Before we talk about crying, and before I explain that bit about Method acting, let's go back a couple of thousand years and meet a distant relative you may not have known that you had—Thespis, the father of all acting.

A Brief History of Acting

Ever since our ancestors started drawing images on the walls of caves, there has been a special place in the world for the storyteller. His stories are about life: shared experiences, death, distant wars, the gods, weather, health—subjects that affect how we survive in this world. Shamans, witch doctors, and medicine men share roots similar to our historical genealogy, but it was in ancient Greece that actors as we know them first appeared. Back then, theatre was a religious thing, a community obligation. Distant tribes would convene in Athens for the Dionysian festivals, which were led by a masked chorus. One day, a member of the chorus—Thespis—donned a mask, pretended to be a god, and spoke back to the chorus. Acting was born. In due time, the solo actor was joined by other actors and, after a couple hundred more years, it evolved that the chorus supported the actors instead of the other way around. (The modern-day Broadway musical still fits this paradigm.) Religious ceremonies morphed into drama as gods were replaced in the stories by demigods, human beings, and heroes. By the time Shakespeare appeared on the British scene in the sixteenth century, drama was focused on man's travails with man rather than his travails with God.

Fade out/fade in to the United States, twentieth century. Stage productions were succeeded by live-action movies, which became a popular and profitable storytelling medium, and by the 1920s, animation started appearing on the big screen, too. I realize some people might disagree with me on the evolutionary steps because I skipped flipbooks and early animation experiments in Europe, but we could debate these fine points all day long. The important thing is that animation is another form of storytelling, and storytelling is an ancient art form that involves actors. Today's animator is an actor. In its modern form, which is what I am concerned with in this book, animation really didn't begin until live-action movies had come to prominence. And now, animation is evolving even further, becoming 3-D. Hand-drawn animation has given way to computer animation, bringing with it sky-high audience expectations and a newly enriched role for the animator/actor. Animation has formally taken its place alongside live-action films and stage plays as a primary storytelling medium, and animators are taking the wand from live actors for the next leg of the race.

Acting for Animators Versus Acting for Actors

The talented animator understands acting theory. The trick is in how he learned it. Animators do not learn acting the same way that actors do. Most of the old-school Disney animators, in fact, were self-taught in acting principles, reading Konstantin Stanislavsky's books and sort of figuring it out for themselves by trial and error. But those were simpler days, and what worked then is increasingly insufficient now. True, there will always be the person who has such raw instinct (for lack of a better word) for acting that he needs no classes. He just "knows." It is true of animators, and it is true of actors. But acting is a craft and an art, and as such is learnable.

Professional acting training is a relatively recent development in history, dating back only to 1897, when Konstantin Stanislavsky established his workshops at Russia's Moscow Art Theatre. It was he, under the influence of Freud and Pavlov, who fathered naturalistic, psychologically based acting techniques. Remember Pavlov's famous experiment with the dog, the food, and the bell? He would ring a bell whenever he fed the dog so, after a while, the dog would salivate when he heard the bell, even if there was no food involved. Stanislavsky observed this and asked himself why actors couldn't do that, too. Would it be possible to train actors to have an emotional reaction to something like a bell ringing? That was the basic idea behind Stanislavsky's work.

Before his innovations, actors struck poses and "showed" the audience that they were experiencing emotion, rather than experiencing the emotion itself. Francois Delsarte (1811–1871), a French teacher of acting and singing, developed a system of acting theory based on poses and physical signals. For example, a character that was under a lot of stress might swoon and place the back of his hand against his forehead to indicate his emotional state. Delsarte's theories were published by Genevieve Stebbins in 1885 as the Delsarte System of Expression and were a popular influence on acting for a short while. Schools such as the American Academy of Dramatic Arts and Emerson's School of Oratory adopted the Delsarte System in the late nineteenth century. Stanislavsky's work totally blew the Delsarte System out of the water, and today Delsarte is little more than an amusing historical footnote in acting theory. An actor practicing the Delsarte System said to the audience, in effect, "I'm not really feeling anything but, if I were, it would look like this." Stanislavsky's response was "Let's really feel something instead of pretending to do so, and let's let our physical gestures be natural expression of emotion."

Before Stanislavsky, acting was learned mainly through a process of informal apprenticeship. An aspiring actor would present himself at the theatre door and ask for the opportunity to learn by doing. He would pull curtains, move props, carry spears in crowd scenes, paint flats, and generally sit at the master's knee, soaking up accumulated theatrical wisdom. When formal acting classes later took root in the

United States and England, the teachers were dependent on this same initiative on the part of the student actor. A student actor was one who wanted badly to be on the stage. In my regular acting classes today, I depend on the student bringing a certain initiative to the process. This is a very significant and important point because it helps explain how acting training for animators is different from acting training for actors. Acting taught to actors in a conventional acting class usually involves a combination of improvisation and scene study. The students memorize scenes, mainly from stage plays, rehearse outside of class and then present the scenes for critique, analysis, and rework. In other words, the student actor gets up and acts.

Since animators do not generally aspire to being on stage themselves, it is nonproductive for an acting teacher to expect them to rehearse and present scenes. Acting training for animators is more akin to acting training for writers or puppeteers. Animators need to have a seat-of-the-pants understanding of acting, but they learn it through observation, discussion, and example rather than workshop scene work and appearances in front of audiences.

Frankly, I think the acting that animators do is more difficult than what actors do. Actors work within the fleeting moment, moving from action to action, emotion to emotion, never looking back, never focusing on the emotion itself. A good animator must go through a similar process of motivating his characters on a moment-to-moment basis, but she then must keep re-creating that same moment over and over and over again, sometimes for weeks on end, while she captures it on the page or computer screen. Actors learn that once a moment is gone, it's gone for good, but animators have to pitch camp at the intersection of movement and emotion. For the actor, it is an error to attempt re-creation of the performance he gave yesterday. For the animator, the ability to re-create—and describe—yesterday's performance is essential.

When an actor rehearses a show, he is not trying to get the performance to a point where it can be frozen and replayed on demand. He is connecting the emotional dots, finding through lines in intention, objectives. The only thing that remains the same on a performance-to-performance basis is the blocking. This is why performances in the theatre are so unique. The audience and the actors get together in the same place at the same time and cocreate the performance. The play your friend saw last week will never be seen again. When you go see the same show on his recommendation, you'll see the same story and blocking, but a different performance. True, an actor's performance can be captured on film but even in that process, the acting happens in the present moment when it's being captured. If an actor does twenty "takes" on a given shot, they are going to be twenty different takes. On a moment-to-moment basis, nothing remains the same. The performance that was captured on film this morning is going to be different from the performance that is captured after lunch. Animators, comparatively speaking, operate in a much different kind of environment.

A book about acting theory—whether for actors or animators—presents a hurdle similar to that encountered by books about mountain climbing, gardening, or skin diving—you can read about acting all you want, but you don't really learn it until you experience it firsthand—which returns us again to that primary distinction between actors and animators: actors actually, for real, *do* it when they are acting. You teach an actor to ride a bicycle by getting him up on the bike and pushing him down the road. Animators actually, for real, *describe* it when they are acting. Many of them don't want to get up on a bicycle in the first place. My goal here is to create a bridge between these two worlds.

Seven Essential
Acting Concepts
1

The late Shamus Culhane correctly pointed out in his wonderful book, *Animation from Script to Screen* (1990), that Disney-style realism is harder to accomplish than more restrictive, stylized cartoons. To adhere to realism is to abide by the laws of physics, weight, and volume. That's why, even if you do not aspire to realistic animation, it still is smart of you to learn what it's all about—and that is why, even though animation takes many different forms, I am mainly concerned with realism in this book. Picasso's earliest paintings were very realistic. Examine his *Nude Study of José Romain* (1895) and *Science and Charity* (1897) and you'll see realism worthy of Michelangelo. He could not have painted *Seated Old Man* (1970) or *Two Women of Algiers* (1955) without first having learned the basics. His cubist work would have been impossible without a firm foundation in realism.

The following concepts are the base on which I build this book. Once we get into it, you'll discover that there is a lot of blending and cross-referencing in acting theory. Frequently, there are two ways to look at the same issue. Before we get into deeper theory and nuance, I'd like you to keep these basic concepts in mind.

1. Thinking leads to movement and emotion. Everything begins with the brain. Life itself is literally measured in brain activity. A person is declared dead not by the cessation of his heartbeat but by the flattening of brain waves. Thinking, awareness, and reasoning are fundamental to all humanity. When you walk down the street, it is your brain that keeps you erect and moving, even if you aren't thinking consciously about each step. Zap the brain, and the human collapses.

Thinking leads to movement and emotion

Emotion is a result of the thinking you do with your brain. It can be defined as an "automatic value judgment." When your lover caresses you, you experience emotions based on your personal values, your experience with past lovers, the way you were raised. When you hear footsteps behind you on a dark street, you experience emotion based on past experience and perceptions of danger. Your sense of danger is a value response. I might feel very threatened by something that doesn't bother you at all. Each person is unique, but all of us have certain traits in common. We all think, and we all experience emotions. Emotions come from thinking.

Write this on your bathroom mirror and read it every morning: "Thinking tends to lead to conclusions; emotion tends to lead to action." I'm not suggesting that thinking never leads to action. You can notice that your shoe is untied and reach down to tie it. In that case, thinking leads to action. You can see a fly buzzing overhead and decide to swat it, and there can be very little emotion expressed. Thinking can lead to action but significant action tends to spring from emotion. I'm talking here of tendencies and, as I'll explain soon, emotions are the lifeline that connect the actor with his audience. In your animation, you should be in pursuit of emotion. The audience wants to know how your characters feel about things.

Let's go back to the example of walking on a dark street and hearing footsteps behind you. Perception of the footsteps is just raw information, right? I hear a sound that I recognize as footsteps: no emotion is involved in that mental process. You perceive sounds behind you and conclude what they are. Thinking in this case leads to a simple conclusion. Now that you know what the sound is, your emotion kicks into play. It's automatic, beyond your immediate control. How do you feel about the sound of footsteps? If you have ever been mugged on a dark street, you're probably going to feel fear. And when you feel fear, you're going to do something about it! Perhaps you'll quicken your pace or tighten your grip on the pepper spray in your pocket. Perhaps you'll consciously choose not to alter your pace because you don't want to communicate to the person behind you that you are afraid. Emotion leads to the action.

In the 1930s, Walt Disney figured out the connection between thinking, emotion, and movement. He learned what Aristotle discovered a couple of thousand years earlier. People don't just move, they move for a reason. "The mind is the pilot," he explained in a famous memo to the studio's resident art teacher, Don Graham. "We think of things before the body does them." This observation, as self-evident as it may seem now, was revolutionary in animation and led directly to the legendary success of Walt Disney Studios. Beginning with Mickey Mouse, Walt understood that thinking, even if subliminal—a wrestler is moving like crazy, but he's not consciously thinking about moving his arms or legs, right?—leads to movement as well as emotion. Walt gave Mickey a brain! And feelings! It was possible to get the audience to *care* about the characters, not just to laugh at them, if they had feelings. Disney's characters would be funny, they would have heart, and they would think.

2. Acting is reacting. Acting is doing. Bill Tytla (*Snow White*) correctly observed that "the pose is a reaction to something." But it is also true that *all* action is a reaction to something. Your car reacts when you hit the gas; your cat reacts when you step on its tail. You react when your cell phone rings or you get a neck massage. Acting is reacting.

Acting is also *doing*. Acting is both doing *and* reacting. Your character may be reacting to an internal thought ("I'm thirsty") or to an external event such as a fire alarm going off ("Let's get out of here!") or to a tasty burger being served up for dinner ("Yum"). The reaction precedes the doing. The traffic light turns red, so what do you *do* about it? You stop the car. You feel a headache coming on, so what do you *do* about it? Take an aspirin. Wile E. Coyote reacts to the fact that Road Runner just foiled him again, and he immediately begins formulating a new plan of attack on the elusive bird. Captain

Acting is reacting; acting is doing

Hook reacts to the tick-tocking of the crocodile by running away. Running away is *doing* something. You see? Note also that each of the examples I'm giving have another component: emotion. First comes emotion, then comes action. First comes a stimulus, then comes action. If you want to show that a character is cold, you first have him react to the temperature—and then he *does* something about it, namely tries to keep warm, perhaps by rubbing his hands together and stamping his feet. How many times have you seen an animated character indicate cold with trembling and chattering teeth? That's weak acting. A person who is cold will *act* to keep warm. The action is in response to the stimulus. Acting is reacting. Acting is doing.

3. *Your character needs to have an objective.* Any time your character is on stage, you should be able to answer the question What is he doing? And what he's doing—his action—should be active, in pursuit of an objective. Your character needs to be doing something 100 percent of the time. Aristotle referred to this as *unity of action*— small actions that lead to a bigger action, or objective. This simple rule lies at the base of all acting theory. An action without a thought is impossible, and an action without an objective is just a mechanical thing, moving body parts. If your character scratches her nose or swats a gnat, that is doing something, but it is not in pursuit of a theatrical objective. Movement may be subsidiary movement, shadow movement, and therefore not relevant to her primary objective—or it may be in pursuit of a theatrical objective.

In the movie *Gold Rush*, Charlie Chaplin wants to impress Georgia, the dance-hall girl, and her friends by hosting them for New Year's Eve dinner. And so he shovels snow to make the money to buy food for a nice dinner. Shoveling the snow and buying the food are *actions*. These actions are in pursuit of an *objective*, namely impressing Georgia. Get it? The objective a character has informs the action. If you're trying to figure out what kind of action your character should be playing, or how he should be playing it, ask yourself what the character's objective is.

Suppose you had created a scenario in which a character pilots a small airplane from Los Angeles to Las Vegas. His objective is to reach Las Vegas. Preparation for the trip involves a series of interrelated, smaller actions, each of which is in pursuit of the objective. When he climbs into the cockpit, he'll make an instrument check, test the brakes, and make sure he has enough fuel for the trip. His actions (checking the instruments, for example) have a purpose, namely to guarantee that he reaches Las Vegas.

Actions pursue objectives, right? Going a little further, let's consider the quality of the actions that are in pursuit of an objective. There are probably dozens of ways to go through an instrument check in preparation to fly. If the character in your story is flying to Las Vegas to marry his girlfriend, there may be a spring in his step, an extra energy in the way he checks those gauges and fuel levels and scans his maps. If, on the other hand, he is going to Las Vegas to attend his father's funeral, his actions will probably

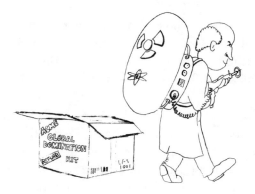

Your character needs to have an objective

have a slower, more determined quality to them, rather than a joyful quality. Movement and emotion live on a two-way street. How you move affects the way you feel; the way you feel affects how you move.

Here's an example of actions pursuing objectives, ripped straight out of today's headlines. In the small California town where I live, residents are in shock over reports that an upstanding local citizen has been arrested and charged with the gruesome murder of his music-teacher wife. According to the records filed with the county court, the man tried to stage the murder scene to resemble an accident, posing his wife's body at the bottom of the basement steps. He wanted to make it seem as though she slipped and fell, striking her head on the way down.

Without getting into more details, we can construct a theatrical scenario from this information already. We pick up the action after the killing, focusing on the staging of the scene to look like an accident. The accused has to do the following, pretty quickly I might add:

1. Clean up the room in the house where the actual killing took place. He has to wash away any incriminating evidence.
2. Change clothes. Put on something that doesn't have bloodspots on it.
3. Dispose of the materials used for cleaning up the crime.
4. Concoct an alibi (if this was not premeditated).
5. Move his wife's body to the bottom of the basement steps.

Each of these steps are actions. And each action is in pursuit of the very strong objective of getting away with murder. He must move quickly, before anybody discovers the body at the bottom of the steps, and he must remain calm to do a thorough job. The context of his situation will influence his mental state, which in turn influences the way he moves.

If you were to animate the part where he's wiping down the walls, you would have to make a decision about how much tension he displays. If the man is a sociopath and has killed before, he will not display as much tension as he would if this was a crime of passion or an accidental (first-time) thing. To be sure, his brain might scramble as he tries to construct an airtight alibi, and this mental effort would show on his face and in his eyes.

You see how it works? First, ask yourself what the character's objective is, then start working on the individual actions. Allow circumstances to affect the manner in which the actions are played.

As long as we are talking about crime, let's consider another murderous example, from the world of Disney animation. When the Evil Queen in *Snow White* is mixing her terrible poisonous brew, her objective is murder. Stirring the pot and occasionally checking with the crystal ball are her actions; killing Snow White is the objective. The Evil Queen isn't nervous because there's no way she can fail! She has magic powers! She's not worried about going to jail, as is our real-life killer, which is probably why the Disney team had her cackle.

And finally, there is the Iron Giant, hurdling through space, intent on detonating the atomic bomb that will otherwise destroy the earth. Flying is his action, and saving the world is his objective. The physical attitude of his flight is a direct result of his desire to be a hero—to do good in the world—like Superman.

4. Your character should play an action until something happens to make him play a different action. Your character should be playing an action 100 percent of the time. During one of my Acting for Animators classes, a student challenged this assertion.

"Suppose he's just sitting there?" she asked. "I think it's possible to just sit around, doing nothing."

Play an action until something happens to make you play a different action

"If someone peeked into this room," I countered, "she could say that you're just sitting around, but you have a purpose in being here. You're sitting in a class, learning about acting because it is going to make you a better animator. Maybe one day, you'll run your own animation studio in part due to what you learn here." Then I asked if anybody in the class could come up with an example from a movie in which a character is doing nothing at all.

"*Toy Story!*" said one fellow with a pretty big grin on his face. "When human characters enter the room, the toys stop moving around and become lifeless toys again. They're not doing anything during that time."

I grinned back. "Nope. Good try, though. Actually, the toys are working very hard to pretend they are lifeless. The premise of the movie is that the toys have a secret life. They live! But it's our little secret, so when humans in the story enter the scene, the toys have to put on the old lifeless-toy act."

Your characters should always be doing something, always moving from action to action.

Keep in mind that the thing that happens to cause your character to play a different action can be internal as well as external. Yes, a human coming into the room motivates a new action for Woody and Buzz. But suppose Woody suddenly remembered where he left his hat? He would move from one action to another, based on an internal stimulus, namely a memory. It's like when you suddenly remember that you left the stove on, just as you're pulling out of the driveway. The thought will cause you to do something about it, namely to repark the car and return to the kitchen to turn off the stove. You play an action until something happens to make you play a different one.

5. All action begins with movement. Even a simple thought is accompanied by movement. Try to multiply 15×92 without moving anything, not even your eyeballs. Can't do it, can you? Heck, you can't even multiply 2×2 without eye movement! Life itself involves movement, even if it is almost imperceptible. Your heartbeat is movement; breathing involves movement. There is movement in life, but we don't usually think much about it. We take it for granted. But now we are talking about theatrical action—action that is in pursuit of an objective. Movement in a theatrical context is more overt than in real life, where a man might sleep under a tree on a sunny day with subtle shiftings.

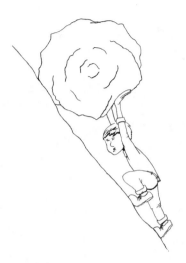

All action begins with movement

We already discussed how acting is doing something (acting is doing; acting is reacting). When you *do* something, you must convert an impulse into something active. Think about it: an impulse is potential action. An impulse is like the string of a bow and arrow, pulled taut. It will not become action until you release the string, sending the arrow toward its target. Actions pursue objectives.

If your character speaks, movement precedes his words. The sequence of events is

1. Think. This may involve an outside stimulus or an inner stimulus. No overt movement is involved.

2. Thinking leads to conclusions, which lead to impulses. No overt movement is involved.

3. Impulses are converted into action. Movement becomes obvious as your character begins to act.

6. Empathy is the magic key. Audiences empathize with emotion. The importance of empathy in acting is a major theme of this book, and I'll spend more time on the subject later.

Empathy is the magic key to acting, because audiences empathize with emotion

For now, just remember this: The basic theatrical transaction is between the actor and the audience, and the thing that holds it all together is emotion. Humans empathize with emotion. The audience is why actors act and why you are animating in the first place. The goal of the animator is to expose emotion through the illusion of movement on screen. What the character is doing on a moment-to-moment basis is vitally important, but the points of empathy with the audience involve emotion, how the character *feels* about what he is doing. Empathy is as essential to dynamic acting as oxygen is to water.

7. A scene is a negotiation. Regular street-variety reality carries zero theatrical voltage. When you walk into a store, there is movement and action all around you—but none of it is theatrical. None is worth the price of admission. People watch movies and stage plays not only for escapism, but also to watch characters working through conflicts. One of the distinguishing elements of a theatrical scene is that it must have conflict—or, as I prefer to put it, every scene must contain a negotiation.

In my acting classes, I frequently see new actors who erroneously believe that acting is about behaving naturally, or believably. While that is partially true, an important concept is lost. Acting involves a contract between actor and audience, and part of the contract demands that what happens on stage has theatrical value. The audience does not show up to watch folks sweep up between shows. They came to watch the show itself. Although, yes, sweeping up involves movement and life and natural behavior, it's not enough to satisfy. Theatrical reality is heightened reality, enhanced and compressed in time and space. (Television commercials are a different matter. We'll get to them later.)

I don't like the word *conflict* much, because it connotes something negative, like a fistfight in a bar, and conflict in acting is not necessarily a negative thing. You can be in conflict about whether to eat the chocolate cake or the apple pie, about whether to vacation in Aruba or Paris. *Obstacle* is a little better, but it still sounds like something soldiers climb during basic training. So, instead of those terms, I prefer to take my lead from playwright David Mamet, who refers to scenes as *negotiations*. A negotiation implies conflict, obstacles, opposing needs—but it suggests a search for a positive resolution. You can negotiate with the car salesman, or you can negotiate with yourself about whether to have a second piece of pie. It is always a good idea to ask yourself what is being negotiated in a scene. If you can't find a negotiation, you've most likely got theatrical trouble.

I have selected these seven concepts mainly because we need to hang our hat somewhere before we get down to work. There are many other acting concepts to consider, but these seven are bedrock.

A scene is a negotiation

Keep them in mind as we move forward, and from time to time, go back and review them. You'll quickly notice that a scene and a character analysis can be viewed from different perspectives. There is a lot of cross-referencing when it comes to acting. For instance, acting is indeed "doing" something. But then, if you are playing an action in pursuit of an objective, you are already "doing" something. It really does not matter which concept comes first, because they both lead to the same place.

The Audience
2

The Actor-Audience Contract

> To be an animator, you have to have a sense of the dramatic, a feeling for acting.
> —Marc Davis, animator of Cruella De Vil in 101 *Dalmatians*

> Everything on the stage must be significant. Even if we are playing the most naturalistic play, everything must be done significantly. The actor must have inside him the feeling of significance at all times.
> —Michael Chekhov, celebrated 1930s actor and acting teacher

In the two quotes above, Marc Davis and Michael Chekhov are talking about the same thing. This "feeling for acting" or "feeling of significance" is one of the least understood and most important aspects of the actor's art, resting on the premise that actors and audience members have an unspoken but ironclad "contract" with one another. The basic terms of the contract call for the actor to assume a leadership, high-status position, to take the audience on a journey, to tell a story. The audience, for its part, plays along, suspending its disbelief in the pretend circumstances on stage. They know the living room walls are actually made out of canvas, that nobody is actually stabbing Julius Caesar, that the actor playing Romeo doesn't really die every night. In effect, the audience presents itself in the theatre and says to the performers on stage, "Take me where you want to. I'm ready to travel!"

If we stick with the notion that the roots of animation can be traced back to ancient theatre and storytelling, then it follows that the animator-as-actor also enters into a contract with the audience. On some level, the audience understands that they're looking at lines and pixels, but because they want to be affected emotionally by what's on the

The actor-audience contract

screen, they pretend that's not so. Now, please understand me on this point: I'm not suggesting that the audience *ever* becomes unaware that they're looking at a cartoon. Just as you always know you're sitting in a movie theatre or in the audience of a play, the audience for animation always knows it is watching animation. But the audience's involvement is emotional. In order for that to happen, the audience has to sort of pretend that the animated characters on screen actually live. It's a kind of secret handshake between the audience and the animator. "Let's pretend together!" is the agreed-upon pact.

When Tinker Bell almost dies in Disney's *Peter Pan*, the people in audience do not mutter, "Aw, heck, it's just a bunch of drawings." Instead, they are likely to start yelling at the screen, "I believe! I believe!" in order to save the fairy. They are holding up their end of the contract, you see? When your character performs, you are saying to the audience, in effect: "I (the animator) think these things about this character are important to the telling of this story." The audience's obligation is to suspend its disbelief and play along with you. The audience relates to the characters on screen, but it communicates with you, the animator. In the final analysis, the transaction involves humans communicating with other humans, not humans communicating with drawn images.

Actors on stage have the benefit of spontaneous feedback from the audience, and they adjust their performance accordingly on a moment-to-moment basis. The experience of live acting is sort of like riding a wave. The actor is on the surfboard; the audience is the current. That's what makes a theatrical event. But the animator is at a major disadvantage when he enters into this actor-audience contract because he does not receive the immediate feedback from his work that an actor on stage does. Instead, he works alone, playing for the audience in his head, which becomes a surrogate for the intended audience. If you are animating for a kid's TV show, you'll make a different kind of performance than you will if you are animating, say, a movie like *Antz*. You do one kind of performance if you are playing for five- to eight-year-old kids and another if you are playing for adults, right? Audiences are not generic, and the audience in your head will take the form of whoever your intended audience is. Broadway actors learn early on that the gray-haired Wednesday matinee audience is a very different animal from the more hip audience that shows up on Friday night. The performance varies with the audience. The audience is the cocreator of the show. The animator, then, is sitting in for the audience that isn't there, the audience as he *imagines* it, and he is guessing at its response. (Playwright Jeffrey Sweet writes eloquently about the actor/audience contract as it applies to theatre in his book *Dramatist's Toolkit: The Craft of the Working Playwright* [1993].)

In order to gain a better understanding of this feeling for acting, I'm going to ask you to play a game with me. Forget for a moment about the happy-go-lucky world of cartoons, and let's go back to the ancient origins of acting. Think of acting as a religious transaction instead of entertainment. Imagine a synagogue or church, a physical layout similar to a legitimate theatre. The audience (congregation) sits in an orderly fashion facing the stage (pulpit). You're the wise leader, the one who decides what the lesson is for today and how the story is going to be told. The audience (congregation) wants to know what you understand about life. They have gotten together in order to experience their humanity. It's a tribal thing. Underneath drama, comedy, and animation, the person on stage is sharing his wisdom and perspective with the audience. The stage is a pulpit.

Okay, that's enough. You can shift your brain back to comedy and the real world now. Can you see what I'm getting at here? When you animate, there ought to be theatrical intention, an awareness of your audience. To hold up your end of the theatrical contract, you must lead the audience. It's not enough to make a character move, he must move for a purpose. A theatrical purpose. Later on we'll talk about the connections between comedy and drama, how they're joined at the hip. For now, just keep in mind that acting has its roots in religion, and the feeling of acting is similar to the feeling of being in the pulpit. We just have more fun.

I read a study a while back in which it was determined that an actor in his first entrance on stage can experience the same blood pressure rise as does a jet aircraft test pilot during takeoff. As an animator, you do not have to personally get up on the stage, but your character does. You get up there vicariously. Because your character acts, and you're the one pulling his strings so to speak, you will experience that adrenaline rush at the first screening of your work. Your character, through you, needs to be thrilled by that same dimming of the house lights that excites actual actors.

Confidence on stage manifests itself in a feeling of "centeredness," certainty. A good actor—or animator—accepts his position in the pulpit, and it makes him feel anchored. That's what the "feeling for acting" Marc Davis speaks of is all about. It's a heightened sense of purpose. The feeling for acting involves knowing that you, through your character, belong on the stage, that you deserve to be there, that you have something worthwhile to say to the audience. It is not enough to merely animate a character, to make him move believably. He must be animated with theatrical intention, theatrical purpose. A moth flying around a lightbulb is animated, but just because there is a lot of wing activity does not make the flight theatrical. Bring in a fly swatter, and you start getting theatre.

Theatrical Reality Versus Regular Reality

The actor-audience contract also requires a certain *kind* of communication. Theatrical reality is not the same thing as regular reality. Regular reality is what you get at the corner grocery store. The theatrical moment—whether on stage or screen, live action or animated—is interpretative: condensed in time and space, designed for maximum impact on the audience. Animation is not supposed to be "real life." It is more than real life. Regular reality is about letting it all hang out; theatrical reality is about letting *some* of it hang out. Flowers in the garden are lovely, but they aren't art. They become art when Monet or Cézanne paints his impression of them. A pair of old shoes is just a pair of old shoes but, by the time Van Gogh gets through with *his* pair of old shoes, we have art. When Charlie Chaplin buys flowers from the blind girl at the beginning of *City Lights*, the

Theatrical reality versus regular reality

moment becomes meaningful beyond the simple reality of the flowers, the girl, or the Little Tramp. Art takes reality to another dimension—one that springs from the artist's brain. The important thing is what Van Gogh *thinks* about his old shoes, what Monet *thinks* about a flower garden, how Chaplin makes a metaphor of the girl's blindness.

Holding the Mirror Up to Nature

Shakespeare said that actors should "hold the mirror up to nature" (Hamlet's advice to the players, Act III, scene 2). What he meant by that is that acting should be a reflection of reality, not reality itself. In order to reflect reality, however, you first have to be acutely aware of it. Hang a camera around your neck; go for a walk through the city streets, and you'll see photographs everywhere you look. Actors have to be like that, but without the camera. Instead of photographs, we are continually taking mental pictures of human behavior. It can be embarrassing for the nonactor companion of an actor when they're out in public because actors will lurk and eavesdrop on even the most personal goings-on. That couple pitching woo in the back booth at the coffee shop deserve their privacy, but their body language is the artist's no-cost classroom—

and so he tunes in as the lovers lock eyes, as she leans forward slightly, and his gaze shifts to her bosom. We watch as he, under the cover of a quiet laugh, reaches across the table and places his hand gently on hers. She responds by adjusting her fingers to grip his. That's reality. The spaghetti-eating scene in *Lady and the Tramp* is an artist's reflection of the reality of lovers at a table.

An actor can be in the middle of a heated argument with his partner, things are going hot and heavy, and inside a happy little voice is whispering to his brain: "This is *good*! You can *use* this!" Absolutely everything in life is fair game for the actor. You never know when you can use your memory of, say, the way a particular street person is digging in a trash can. Watch how he retrieves that partially empty raspberry jam jar, checks the label, and deciding that he prefers grape or orange marmalade, returns it to the trash. Yep, that's one I've been carrying around with me for twenty years. The old guy was rummaging in a trash can situated at 72d and Broadway in New York City, and one day I'll use it.

Someone may have observed it earlier, but Aristotle was the first person I know of who pointed out in the *Poetics* that we humans learn by imitating what we see. Stick your tongue out at a baby, and she'll stick hers out at you. Boys learn how to shave by watching Dad; we all learn the alphabet and arithmetic through a process of imitation. Next time you see a person involved in a conversation fold his arms across his chest, notice whether or not the person he is talking to also does that. Most times, he or she will. We imitate one another a lot. It's part of our human nature. A drawing or an image on celluloid is a representation of real life. We humans experience pleasure in the very act of identifying it as such. When the drawing or image on screen moves and talks, seemingly expressing emotion, we delight in the recognition of our own feelings. Theatrical reality is a copy of reality, which has been highlighted and emphasized in whatever ways the artist deems appropriate in order to communicate his perspective to the audience.

Character

3

Personality Animation

Personality. That is the key, the drum, the fife. Forget the plot. Can you remember, or care to remember, the plot of any great comedy? Chaplin? Woody Allen? The Marx Brothers?

—Chuck Jones in *Chuck Amuck*

The movements and attitudes of a figure should display the state of mind of him who makes them, and in such a way that they cannot mean anything else.

—Leonardo da Vinci

Which is more important: character (personality) or action? Can you have one without the other? Walt Disney was obsessive about personality. Shamus Culhane contends it is personality first, personality second, and personality third when it comes to animation. Many legendary animators, in fact, refer to the necessity for characters to have colorful personalities. That's all well and good, but what *is* personality? How does one create personality? We all understand that Mickey Mouse has a winning and delightful personality, but what does that mean precisely?

The key to personality is action. Personality is expressed through action. Indeed, personality that is *not* expressed through action is nothing at all. Dead men don't tell tales, and they don't have personalities. Personality is inherent in action, and action is inherent in life. Roy Rogers' horse, Trigger, had a marvelous personality when he was running around in the old Republic westerns, but today he stands stuffed in a southern California museum. No personality there except in the memory of people who remember him from the movies.

A thought by itself is just a thought. It's not even a smile. A tendency to blush is a personality trait, but it's not relevant unless the character moves. When you animate a character, you are expressing its thoughts and emotions through the illusion of movement, or action. The movement can be as slight as the tightening of a gaze (Clint Eastwood has made a career of this, in fact) or a Mona Lisa smile, but there must be movement if the character's thoughts are to mean anything to an audience. And the *way* the character's thoughts are expressed amounts to its personality. Miss Piggy, my all-time favorite character on *Sesame Street*, has a strong personality because she is so self-centered, but her character description won't matter unless she *acts* in a superior manner. She's the star of her own show in life, and she casts everybody else in the world as supporting players.

Aristotle wrote in the *Poetics* that actions are performed by persons who must have qualities of character and mind. Character and thought, said he, are the two natural causes of action. It is through action that men succeed or fail. We act to live, and we live to act. Walt Disney, in that famous 1935 memo to Don Graham, said "in most instances, the driving force behind the action is the mood, the personality, the attitude of the character—or all three." So which is it? Is action driven by character and thought, as Aristotle said, or by mood, personality, and attitude, as Disney determined? I submit that Walt had it right to a degree, but Aristotle understood the motivating process at a deeper level. We move in order to survive. What Walt was really talking about was the *quality* of movement rather than the *motive* behind movement. The "driving force" behind movement is an impulse to survive—an evolutionary current, a primal kick. But the *way* a character moves is a factor of mood, personality, and attitude.

If an animator follows only Disney's analysis, he runs the risk of creating a character with a terminal case of the cutes. We are able to discern personality by the way a character moves. It's not like the personality exists in limbo, as a separate entity. The idea of *personality* only makes sense as it relates to movement, and movement is an effort to survive in the world.

Personality in animation began with Disney's *Three Little Pigs* and really came into its own with the seven dwarfs in *Snow White*. True, Winsor McCay's Gertie the Dinosaur had a personality of sorts, but it was primitive compared to the three little pigs. Friz Freleng explains that, in the earliest days of animation, it was enough just to make the characters move—"make 'em walk, make 'em run, make 'em turn around, make 'em talk to each other, in pantomime, of course. But you didn't distinguish one from another; they all did it the same. But when Walt got into distinguishing one from another by personalities, then it changed the whole thing" (Merritt and Kaufman 2000, 81).

One of the projects I have on my to-do list is to write a children's book featuring a young black Palo Alto squirrel who is afraid of heights. As soon as I introduce the fear-of-heights character trait, the squirrel's personality will begin to form. An animator would know that the squirrel will move differently when he's on the ground than he will when he's in a tree or balancing an elevated telephone line above the traffic. His body language will change if he even *thinks* about climbing a tree! (If you can draw a pretty good squirrel and are interested in collaborating with me on this project, send an e-mail.) The point is that, when we speak of personality, we are speaking of the way a particular character behaves, the way he *acts*.

Character Analysis

Fred Moore's character and personality analysis of Mickey Mouse, as presented in *The Illusion of Life: Disney Animation* (Thomas and Johnston 1981) goes like this:

> Mickey seems to be the average young boy of no particular age; living in a small town, clean living, fun-loving, bashful around girls, polite and as clever as he must be for the particular story. In some pictures he has a touch of Fred Astaire; in others of Charlie Chaplin, and some of Douglas Fairbanks, but in all of these there should be some of the young boy. (551)

That's all, folks. That's the total character analysis of Mickey Mouse.

Fred Moore was, of course, one of the giants of animation, a certified pioneer, and his analysis of Mickey was sufficient for its day. Indeed, he was one of the first to point out that cartoon characters could be made to think. I am not about to criticize Fred Moore, but the complicated 3-D characters that are being created by animators today cannot get by with such a simple character analysis. Note how almost every reference in Moore's analysis of Mickey is a generality: "no particular age," "average young boy,"

Character analysis

"a small town," "as clever as he must be for the particular story." *Which* small town? East or west? Probably midwest, similar to Walt's origins, but it wasn't spelled out. What the heck *is* an "average young boy" anyway?

Audience expectations are higher than they used to be when it comes to animation, and an in-depth character analysis is essential whether you are animating a preexisting character or creating a character of your own. Glen Keane, one of the elite character animators of today (*The Little Mermaid, Tarzan*), prepared a nine-page analysis of *The Little Mermaid* character Ariel when that Disney film was in production, and his notes have fortunately found their way into the public domain (<http://www.iserv.net/~ lbarron/arieljas.html>). This website is maintained by Jay Barron, a self-described freelance illustrator and animation fan. Mr. Barron explains that "part of this [analysis] appeared in Disney's Little Mermaid Comic #1" and that "the document is copyrighted in part by the Walt Disney Company." The analysis includes personality description, character history, and physical description. You will immediately see how dramatically times have changed since Fred Moore's description of Mickey Mouse.

Note how specific Glen Keane is. Ariel is the youngest of seven daughters and is sixteen years old! Not fourteen or eighteen, but sixteen. Her fiery side, "red hair and all," is balanced by her sweetness. She is naïve and innocent. Mr. Kean's analysis is to Mr. Moore's analysis is like what a 747 jet liner is to a Steerman.

You can no longer just say a character is cute and cuddly and has a great personality, especially if you expect it to carry a lead role in a feature film or television series. What might work for the less discriminating audience of a computer game will not work for the average moviegoers. It makes a difference if the character you're animating is from San Francisco or the Bronx, if he's thirteen instead of sixteen years old, if he likes to play basketball more than he likes to play chess, if he's shy around girls.

And you'll be surprised how character elements that may never be mentioned or used in your animation can still provide strong motivation. For example, the story line of your script may include no reference to romance, may in fact include no romantic scenes at all, but it is still a good idea for you to know precisely how the characters procreate (here, I'm presuming nonhuman characters). If evolutionary theory is correct, and if a species acts to propagate itself, then *all* character activity—even if it is not explicitly about making the beast with two backs—will serve that ultimate objective. In other words, even though you may lay out a very complex and complete character analysis and description, that does not mean you have to make all of those character traits visible.

Let's create a couple of characters—one human and one nonhuman. Think of a character analysis as a biography.

Human Character Analysis

Male or female?

Age?

Physical health?

Appearance? Hygiene?

Intelligence?

Diet?

Culture?

History?

Religion?

Income?

Occupation?

Education?

Sexual orientation?

Family?

Friends?

Inner rhythm?

Psychology (introvert, extrovert, etc.)?

Goals?

Name

From this I can decide that our human character will be a female, seventeen years old, whose name is Jasmine Franco. She is a second-year student at the university in Siena, Italy, and is in excellent physical health, except for occasional stiffness in her left leg, a result of a motor scooter accident four years ago. She is the first child of Gianna and Sergio, and she has a younger brother, Osvaldo, who still lives at home. Jasmine is extremely bright and wants to do everything in life. Sometimes she aspires to be an attorney, other times she wants to be an economist but, when she is allowing her dreams to take over, what she really, in her heart wants, is to be an archaeologist. Her hobby is history, and she enjoys nothing more than volunteering on historical excavations. Most recently, she participated in a dig in Sicily. Her boyfriend, Paulo, transferred from the university in Siena to one in London at the end of the last school year, which has resulted in very high telephone charges for her parents, who live in Rome, a four-hour drive south of Siena. Jasmine is as graceful as a gazelle, even regal; 5'9" tall, has alert gray-blue eyes, thick straw-colored hair, and is extremely popular with her friends. She is multilingual, speaking Italian, French, and English. She projects an outward air of calm and humor, which disguises an inner restlessness and a melancholy, poetic streak.

Now for our nonhuman creature.

Nonhuman Character Analysis

Physical attributes? (Keep in mind evolutionary necessity)

Locomotion? (Normal humans walk, snakes slink, Superman flies)

Age?

Life span?

Diet?

Physical health? Physical handicaps? Lost a leg? Hard of hearing?

How does he procreate?

Defense mechanism?

Relatives?

Sense of humor?

Fears?

Goals?

Culture?

Intelligence?

Education?

Relationship to other characters in story?

Source of income? Livelihood? Industry?

Name?

Ferd-Ferd is roughly two hundred human years old but is just a youngster in Sklar time. He's two-and-a-half feet tall when he stands straight up, but of course that is an unnatural posture for him, angling forward as he does. Anyway, when he stands straight up, it causes his receptor eye to dangle uncomfortably. He is bald, as are all Sklartons, and his soft outer shell is still an adolescent, healthy (and dangerously visible) translucent green. Sklartons don't go to school but are educated in the irradiating bin while they're in the larval stage. This encodes them with knowledge enough for their early life survival, provides them with a job description, and will successfully sustain most of them when they endure the Predylactus Feast. It's definitely not an easy life being a primary food source for the Predylactus but Ferd-Ferd nonetheless must make his adult migration to the Elucian Caves in order to mate. Already he is worrying about the upcoming journey, but there is no turning back. Until the dreadful day of departure, Ferd-Ferd will spend his time cultivating life-sustaining Sklar mold back in the rear chamber of the enclave. It's pretty much all work and no play for Sklar youngsters, but Ferd-Ferd and his buddies are always getting into trouble with their pranks.

Remember: What the audience sees on stage is just the tip of the iceberg. Eighty percent of what is happening to a character is under the surface, tied up in context, character background, given circumstances. It's not all "shown." For example, a man walks into an office, having been summoned there by his boss. He brings with him the circumstances of his life, right? Maybe his wife told him just this morning that she is pregnant, or maybe he has been leaving work early for months and is fearful that the boss has finally found out about it. Maybe he has a bunion on his foot, or a headache. All of these things affect what goes on as he enters the room even though they aren't shown on the screen.

Primal Analysis

> Bugs is simply, and only, trying to remain alive in a world of predators.
> —Chuck Jones in *Chuck Amuck*

> The theme of life is conflict and pain. Instinctively, all my clowning was based on this.
> —Charlie Chaplin

Trying to figure out what makes people tick is a constant challenge and delight for me as it is for most actors, and my opinions in that department strongly color my views on acting. In particular, there are two psychological approaches to acting that I use frequently: the primal analysis and Carl Jung's concept about anima and animus, masculine and feminine.

A primal analysis will help you tap into a commonly shared stream of human values, leading you toward empathic acting choices. It seems self-evident to me that one way or the other we humans must propagate ourselves or die out as a species. Therefore, when I'm holding that mirror up to nature, I tend to view human behavior as a humongous mating dance, one that is not always graceful. It can be very empowering when an actor finds a strong primal stream for his character. It can sometimes open up a scene or story in unforeseen ways, and it will often explain a character's baffling behavior. At a minimum, it can help differentiate needs from wants, and needs are always more powerful motivators acting-wise.

For example, in the Tennessee Williams play *A Streetcar Named Desire*, Blanche is in primal competition with her younger, pregnant sister Stella. She struggles throughout the play to appear and behave younger than she is, relying frequently on special effects, the soft flattering light cast by paper lanterns. She tries unsuccessfully—and with increasing desperation—to get local bachelor Mitch to propose to her, but her sexual energy is directed toward Stanley, her sister's husband. Stanley is coarse and simple, a graceful apelike boy/man who is possessed of extraordinary magnetism. Blanche is highstrung, nervous, painfully aware that her biological clock is ticking, and her Old South, plantation values are in conflict with the modern world. In the end, when Blanche can no longer hide her real age, her dark past, or her agenda, when she is forced into the harsh light of day instead of that cast by the Chinese lanterns, she literally implodes, experiencing a nervous breakdown and institutionalization. Before she is escorted to the hospital, however, Blanche and Stanley finally have their sexual day of reckoning.

What draws Blanche to Stanley? We're not talking about teenage passion here, kids tumbling around in the back seat of the Chevy, but something considerably deeper and more complex. Blanche, increasingly unanchored as the story progresses, longs for Stanley's strength, his certainty. It's primal.

The world of animation is full of good examples of primal motivation. Think of Tramp's courtship of Lady in *Lady and the Tramp*, Popeye's love for Olive Oyle, Tarzan's courtship of Jane. In classical drama, Anthony literally went to war because of his lust for Cleopatra, and Romeo ultimately gave his life for love of Juliet. When Medea, bent on revenge against her husband, Jason, murders her own children as an act of revenge, her crime is almost a dictionary definition of primal motivation. Though she never says it out loud, the Medea principle is that, if you kill a man, you kill him once. But if you kill his children, you kill him repeatedly—again and again and again. Medea's man abandoned her, and so she struck back by killing his children. It is no mystery to me why this story of a woman scorned continues to shock audiences two thousand years after Euripides wrote it.

Two more examples from the world of animation: the queen in *Snow White* and Cruella De Vil in *101 Dalmations*. The queen is, to me, not merely a vain woman with an "envious heart." She is of a certain age and has an evolutionary interest in being the fairest one in the land. When her magic mirror informs her that she is not the fairest in the land, she obsesses on the demise of lovely, fertile Snow White. It's never made clear who the queen and Snow White are competing for, manwise—neither in the Grimm's fairy tale nor in the Disney movie—but the possibilities are intriguing and perhaps disturbing, given that the Queen is Snow White's step-mother. The most important point, in my view, is that their competition is primal. The queen is not just *choosing* to destroy Snow White, she's *driven* to do so. She's not a serial killer. The object of her fury is very specific, a young, lovely woman of childbearing age. Again, it's primal.

Cruella De Vil has a similar problem with her vanity. Why does she lust for a puppy-skin coat? Surely, it must be because she believes that wearing one will make her more attractive. Even though she is married, a puppy-skin coat will perhaps bring her more attention. One of a kind, and all that. Marriage does not stop men and women from wanting to appear attractive to the opposite sex, and this is really the only explanation that makes any sense about Cruella's obsession. The actor's job is to make sense of the character. It's not enough to write off Cruella as an oddball. Oddballs don't think they are oddballs. There must be a reason for a character's behavior, something that drives him, and the more specific the better. In the cases of Cruella and the Evil Queen, a primal analysis fits. They are both being pushed along in life, fighting against age, dancing the mating dance, almost like salmon swimming upstream. Neither of them can help themselves.

The justification for a primal analysis is closely related to the mechanisms of empathy. It is not an optional matter that we propagate ourselves. We're wired that way by nature. We *need* to propagate. It is a driving, motivating force behind virtually all human behavior. And, since it is true that humans will respond emotionally to the emotions of other humans, you as an animator are digging in a very rich vein when you find the primal motivation. Most of us don't relate much to the emotions of a sociopath or serial killer because the psychology of such a person is abnormal. But we all do the mating dance, one way or the other, for better or worse, dignified or awkward, and so we all recognize the emotions that the dance brings out in characters on screen. Tex Avery, for one, got a lot of mileage out of this fact of life with his insanely lusting, pop-eyed, leering characters.

I understand that applying a primal analysis is not for everybody, and may even be considered politically incorrect by some, and I'm not suggesting that this is the only way to look at things. I won't stand in fire to argue with those who contend that evolutionary theory is a crock. If you are a person who figures that the biological clock is overplayed, that males and females have the same psychology, and the human mating dance is a figment of a sexist, uninformed out-of-date imagination, you have a lot of company. This is a book about acting technique, not sociology and, acting-wise, whatever works is okay. I simply feel that I would be remiss not to share this perspective because it has worked so well for me over the years, and it provides a compass for my orientation to acting. It's a tool, a technique you can call on when you don't know what else to do. Actors learn early on that there is no single carved-in-stone way to approach a character. The idea is to stimulate yourself one way or another, to find points of empathy with the audience. The value in the primal approach is that it can put you in touch with what the character *needs* rather than what he *wants*. And need has more theatrical voltage, is a more common currency, than want.

The main principles that support a primal analysis are as follows:

1. We humans act to survive.

2. If we are to survive, we must propagate ourselves.

3. Life is a big mating dance, and it's not always pretty.

4. The female has a genetic incentive to seek Mr. Right, to find a mate who will make a strong commitment—financially and physically—to her and their offspring.

5. The male usually is monogamous, but has a genetic incentive to seek many mates.

6. The female biological clock is real. Without medical intervention, there comes a time in a woman's life cycle when she can no longer bear children.

7. Males have no biological clock. They will therefore dance the mating dance right up to the midnight hour.

8. Though a woman may *choose* not to have children, nature will still very likely push her in the childbearing direction. The closer a woman is to the far edge of her biological clock, in fact, the stronger nature's push will influence her life choices. A woman who is pushing forty, for example, tends to be less understanding about a man in her life who will not make a serious commitment to her.

Evolutionary psychology teaches that "emotions are just evolution's executioners" (Wright 1994, 88). What that means is that we are hard-wired to feel good about things that are good for propagating our species, like sex. We like sex because it is good for us. And we are hard-wired *not* to like things that are bad for us, like infanticide and incest. Observe that the idea of infanticide—a parent killing his or her own child—causes you to feel more disgusted than the idea of a serial killer does. Remember the Susan Smith child-drowning incident in North Carolina in the early 1990s? She strapped her two young sons into their car seats and pushed the car into a lake. The case created a firestorm of press coverage. I always saw Susan Smith as a Medea figure, though she was portrayed in the press in a different light. The public wanted to string her up for having killed her two children in that lake. Internet chat rooms and Letters to the Editor sections of newspapers were buzzing with calls for her slow torture, preferably by water. Now, compare the public's reaction to Susan Smith with the reaction to another highly publicized criminal, Jeffrey Dahmer. Here was a serial killer that liked to dismember his victims and eat them! Dahmer was the topic of jokes on late-night talk shows, but you never heard a single joke about Susan Smith. Why? Because infanticide is a no-no. It's bad for our species. Mothers are not supposed to kill their own children, and the public simply does not find it funny. Nature wires mothers to nurture and care for their children and, when this goes awry, it is extremely disturbing to most of us. But Dahmer was just a garden variety, sociopathic murderer in the vein of Hannibal Lecter in *Silence of the Lambs*.

All humans act to survive. The first thing we do when we are born is try to live, and the last thing we do before we die is try to live. And we have to propagate ourselves if we are going to continue living for another generation. It is this shared survival mechanism that is at the heart of the empathic response. And remember, as artists we are in pursuit of empathy, not sympathy. When you feel sympathy for someone, you simply feel sorry for him and may or may not empathize. When you feel empathy, you identify with him. A primal analysis leads directly to the empathic response.

Playing the Opposite: Masculine/Feminine

Perhaps Carl Jung's most lasting contribution to the study of psychology was his idea that, underneath the masculine personality, there is a feminine side (*anima*) and, underneath the feminine personality, there is a masculine side (*animus*). He taught that the masculine side is the more analytical, cerebral part; the feminine side is more sensitive, nurturing, intuitive. All of us humans have both, according to Jung, and one side is not superior to the other (Hopcke 1989, 45). Although Jung's theory invites sexual stereotyping and was developed in an era of regressive sexual context, it nonetheless can be an empowering tool for actors if used judiciously.

An actress in my scene study workshop was having difficulty portraying Medea. She simply could not imagine a situation in which she might kill her own children and was not relating to the character. Mothers just don't kill their own children! After the actress had gone through half a dozen unsuccessful attempts at a crucial monologue from the play, in which Medea explains and justifies her crime, I suggested that she operate out of the masculine side of her personality. Bingo! The improvement was immediate because the actress released herself from the nurturing-mother impulses that live within her and tapped into her more aggressive masculine side. Infanticide runs counter to the way we are wired by nature, particularly for women. From that actress' perspective, a woman wouldn't murder her own children, but a man might do it. When the actress shifted to the masculine side of herself, the balance within her shifted so that vengeance became much more focused than nurturing. It became more an act of calculation, of war. No audience would ever have known what this actress was using internally to make the external moment work for her, nor did it matter. In acting, anything that works is fair.

Another example from one of my acting classes: Two actresses were working on the mother/daughter scene from Shaw's play *Mrs. Warren's Profession*. The actress playing the mother was having difficulty because, in this particular scene, her daughter spurns her financial support and banishes her forever from her sight. The daughter is motivated to take this drastic action because she has learned that her mother earned her fortune by running prostitution houses. It is dirty money. The daughter is rejecting her mother's values, even though it was her mother's money that paid for the better education she received, the education that resulted in the development of values she is now turning on her mother.

The actress playing the mother related much more to the nurturing aspect of motherhood than the hardball attributes necessary for running a house of prostitution. In the scene, she was grief-stricken by her daughter's rejection, and she allowed herself to be verbally manhandled. From beginning to end, she was backpedaling, beseeching her daughter not to do this awful thing. The net result was that the scene was not interesting. It contained no negotiation the way they were playing it. Daughter advances, mom retreats. In order to make it work, the mother would have to advance, and the daughter would have to retreat, at least some of the time. The actual dialogue of Shaw's script would allow this interpretation.

And so I suggested to the actress that she get more in touch with the part of herself that is capable of operating prostitution houses. "Suppose you were running a house and one of your girls was upstairs, being beat up by a customer. What would you do?" "I'd go up there and kick him out!" "Exactly. I believe that is what you would do. But that requires a lot of strength and courage and has nothing whatever to do with nurturing anybody. In other words, you have to operate out of the more masculine side of your personality if you are going to be a successful madam. Now, in this scene with your daughter, it will help if you are not as torn apart by her rejection, if you are looking for ways to thrust and parry with her. We need a negotiation. You need to be giving as good as you get. If you are just the hurt and nurturing mom, we won't get it." They did the scene again, and this time the daughter had to contend with a capable, strong, self-reliant woman who was her mother. It worked like gangbusters.

Cruella De Vil operates a lot out of her masculine side, it seems to me. If there is any nurturer in her, it is well hidden, that's for sure. She pursues her goal of a puppy-skin coat with as much zeal as Patton pursued the enemy in WWII. Stanley Kowalski in Tennessee Williams' play, *A Streetcar Named Desire,* is a brute of a character on the surface. He drinks too much, carouses with the boys too much, beats up his wife, sabotages Mitch's romance with Blanche, and, as a final violent act, actually rapes Blanche. And yet Marlon Brando played this character in a way that made us care deeply about Stanley's needs and his insecurities. He made us empathize with this man/boy, this man's man with the vulnerability of a woman. Elia Kazan directed both the original stage production and the subsequent movie, which also starred Brando. He offers this assessment of Brando's work:

> Brando made Stanley petulant. He wants everything his own way. If he doesn't get it, he'll either beat you up or he'll cry. How many times have you seen that in your rough friends? The beat the hell out of their wives, and the next minute they're apologizing. (Young 1999, 84)

This fits the masculine/feminine analysis, hard and soft, mean and sweet, rought and tender, assertive and needy.

The primal analysis and the masculine/feminine contrast are nothing more than tools. In acting terms, we call them *techniques*, which means, what you use when you don't know what else to do. You're looking at a blank page, a character that somehow just won't live. If you can discover a primal stream, or Jungian opposites, or negotiations within the scene, or if you can convert the character's wants (optional) to needs (essential), you might be able to get your creative fire going.

One is not a better technique than the other, nor is any one of these approaches essential. As I have said before, when it comes to acting, you use what works for you at the time. And the fact that it may work for you this time is no guarantee that it will work as well for you the next time. What matters is that your characters project their personalities through their actions, and that these actions are consistent with their respective personalities.

The Scene

4

A movie or a play is comprised of scenes. One scene relates to another and all together the scenes add up to the story being told. But what is a scene exactly? What is the difference between a scene in a movie and, say, dinner conversation between you and your in-laws? And if you are given a scene to animate, what can you do to bring it to life?

Let's start here: Acting is an interpretive art. When we act, we are telling a story, presumably one with a point. When we tell the story it's in a hierarchical fashion—point A leads to point B leads to point C leads to the conclusion of the story. This is the main difference between that dinner conversation I mentioned and a scene in a movie. A dinner conversation isn't related to a larger story, nor is it a step along the way to anything. It is what it is—a pleasant way to spend some time. And anyway, nobody is paying admission to watch you and your in-laws eat dinner. A theatrical scene, on the other hand, has significance and relevance to the larger story being told. The actors are leading a willing audience on a journey.

Stanislavsky's system dictated that scenes tell the story of a play the same way a musical score organizes sound. Actors play *actions*, which are designed to solve *problems* that are set forth by the *given circumstances* of the play (Carnicke in Hodge 2000, 24).

A theatrical scene can conveniently be thought of as a negotiation. I was delighted to pick up this notion from a talk playwright David Mamet gave at the Writer's Guild in New York some years ago, and I have kitchen-tested it many hundreds of times in my regular acting classes since then. It is definitely easier for actors to grasp the dynamics of a scene if they think in terms of negotiations rather than in the classic ways of either *conflict* or *obstacles*. In a nutshell, when a scene lacks a negotiation, it is guaranteed to fail.

But let's talk for a minute about *conflict* before we switch terminology over to *negotiation*. In acting, there are only three possible kinds of conflict:

1. The character can have conflict with another character. "Your money or your life," threatens the thief.

2. The character can have conflict with herself. "I'm crazy for this man, but he is married! I should not be dating him!" she says to herself as she applies her lipstick.

3. The character can have conflict with the situation in which he finds himself. "Here is neither bush nor shrub to bear off any weather at all, and another storm is brewing!" cries Trinculo in Shakespeare's *Tempest*, caught in a tropical storm. (His resolution is to find shelter near Caliban.)

In a scene, there should always be conflict of some sort. The can be one type of conflict, or there can be two or more types of conflict going on at the same time.

As I mentioned in the first chapter, I don't like the term *conflict*, because of its negative-sounding connotation, nor *obstacle*, which seems trivial and easily traversed. That's why I embrace the idea of the scene as a negotiation. A negotiation contains conflict, or obstacles, but it suggests a transaction in search of a positive resolution. And positive resolutions are, in my view, life affirming, seeking survival. And survival taps back into the primal stream, which I spoke of in the last chapter. You see how it all fits together?

The Fairy Godmother negotiates with Cinderella when she places a midnight curfew on Cinderella's party plans. When Peter Pan saves Tinker Bell's life after she drinks the poison, it is with a condition—a negotiation, if you will. He asks children everywhere to clap their hands if they believe in fairies. Presumably, if the claps were not forthcoming, it would be curtains for Ms. Bell. In *Toy Story*, when Woody agrees to rescue Buzz Lightyear, who has fallen out of the window, the decision involves a negotiation with himself and with the other toys, all of whom are accusing Woody of killing Buzz.

When a scene is giving you trouble, when it feels too shallow, too clownish, when the characters seem to be just making funny faces, stop and look for the negotiation. This can be a marvelously effective litmus test for what is wrong (or right) with a scene.

Status Negotiations

We negotiate status with one another continually, all day long, in all kinds of relationships and interactions. When you go into a restaurant and order a meal, the waiter accords you high status because you are the customer, and he is serving you. There is nothing demeaning about it. This is simply the way the status transaction is playing out at that moment. When you are having a simple conversation with a friend, you accord her high status when you allow her to speak; she returns the favor when she listens to you speak. And there are the more blatant kinds of status transactions between parents and their children, husbands and wives, jailers and inmates, between bosses and secretaries. You are reading this book and, by doing so, you are according me high status, at least for the moment. When a teacher lectures a class, the students are granting her high status. When actors are on stage, the audience is granting them high status.

In order to use this notion of status transactions, you should remove any judgments about it. Status transactions are not usually discriminate, although they could be used that way; they are mainly a way of negotiating interpersonal relationships. Anthony Hopkins used status transactions overtly when he played the butler in the movie *Remains of the Day*. The trick, he said in an interview, was to keep in mind that, from the butler's perspective, all of the space in the room belongs to the master. Whenever Hopkins entered the room, he did so with tacit permission from his master. Observe how a butler helps his master get dressed. He will step into his master's space, presumably by invitation, help him on with his coat—and then step back out! There is a continual acknowledgment on the part of both parties that the master owns the space, and the butler is there to serve. No insults intended. It's a status transaction. Charlie Chaplin used status transactions frequently. When a lower-status character, like the Little Tramp, behaves in a high-status way, maybe putting his feet up on the desk and puffing on a cigar, it is funny.

I have achieved remarkable success in workshop scenes by making nothing more than a simple status adjustment. You can do it, too, in your animation. Give one of your characters higher status than the other, and see what happens. The playground bully, for example, is always trying to stake out high status in his dealings with other characters.

This notion of status negotiations within a theatrical scene is a cornerstone of Keith Johnstone's approach to improvisation, as outlined in his funny and invaluable book, *Impro*. It is such a simple idea that when you first encounter it, you wonder why you didn't figure this out yourself. I had already been acting twenty years before I read *Impro* and was instantly impressed with Johnstone's insight. Probably because I was locked into pejorative thinking about the word *status* (which I related to lower or higher standing in the world, racism, bigotry, and such) that I didn't realize this truth: that a low-status person in a transaction can very well be a high-status person in life. I recommend you read Johnstone's book, and am certain you'll use his concepts in your work.

Starting in the Middle

Playwrights and screenwriters learn to enter scenes as late as possible. Audiences are smart and can fill in the missing blanks. Indeed, the scene will be more interesting for the audience this way. You don't need, for instance, to show a character entering the building and then walking up the stairs before he knocks at the apartment door—unless, of course, you want to make a specific point about him climbing the stairs. Instead of all that, you can begin the scene with the person in the apartment answering the door. Or, you could have the person already in the apartment, and you could pick up the dialogue midconversation, maybe with the characters sitting on the sofa in the living room.

Actors operate on a similar principle, namely that a scene does not begin when the lights come up on stage. It begins offstage, where the "moment before" is created. And the scene will not end when the lights fade to black. When an actor is standing in the wings, waiting for his cue to enter, he is connecting with where he (his character) has been, how he came to be standing just outside the entrance to the stage set, and what his intention is when he enters.

In the Neil Simon play *Barefoot in the Park*, the newlyweds live on the upper floor of a walk-up brownstone. Whenever the husband enters the apartment, he is out of breath from having climbed all those stairs. That is a "moment before." And even more: He may have climbed the stairs wearily or in a head-over-heals hurry, depending on the circumstance, which will also affect the way he enters the scene. Another example: The lights come up on a living room set. A telephone rings. A fellow with a towel around his waist and an annoyed demeanor comes into the living room and answers the telephone. We presume—by filling in the blanks—that he came from the bathroom. If his hair is dripping wet, we presume he got out of the shower to answer the phone. And after he completes his telephone call, exiting in the direction he first entered from, we presume he is returning to the shower. If he exits in another direction, we might presume he is going to the kitchen, if we have already been made aware of the apartment floor plan.

Remember: Your character enters a scene with intention, comes from somewhere else, presumably a previous scene, and will be continuing on to some other scene after he leaves this one. This ties in with the lesson about playing an action until something happens to make you play a different one. A character should always be doing something.

Rehearsal

After an actor is cast in a role, he goes into rehearsal. After an animator is cast on a film or television show, he goes into preproduction. In terms of the development of a character and preparation for performance, I think actors have an advantage over animators. In rehearsal the actor has the opportunity to work all day long with the director and other actors in the cast, experimenting with various approaches to his role. This process can go on for weeks, or even months in the case of a big-budget Broadway show. During rehearsal, the cast is trying to find the beats, rhythm, and tone of the play, the ebb and flow of tension within scenes. An actor may have an idea about how his character should be played, but that can fly right out the window if it doesn't work when put against what the *other* actors in the cast are doing. Preparing a show for opening night in the theatre is an intense process, the very definition of group collaboration. Everybody knows when opening night is, and rehearsal consists of working things out against the imagined response of the probable opening night audience. For the animator, this is the rough equivalent of working in your own head for that audience.

A director understands that an audience must be touched emotionally if a play is to succeed, so a lot of the rehearsal process is actually devoted to finding those emotional triggers or, as I like to call them, *points of empathy*.

Good animation is also dependent on finding points of empathy, and even though animators do not enjoy the same sort of free-flowing rehearsal process, I place this discussion of empathy under the general heading of Rehearsal, because the animator/actor needs to know this stuff before she can give a solid performance.

Emotion and Empathy

[Those] animators will have to be able to put across a certain sensation or emotion . . . for that is all we are trying to do in animation.
—Bill Tytla, Disney animator, speaking to one of Don Graham's Action Analysis classes

Our goal . . . is to make the audience feel the emotions of the characters, rather than appreciate them intellectually. We want our viewers not merely to enjoy the situation with a murmured "Isn't he cu-ute?" but really to feel something of what the character is feeling. If we succeed in this, the audience will now care about the character and about what happens to him, and that is audience involvement. Without it, a cartoon feature will never hold the attention of its viewers.
—Frank Thomas and Ollie Johnston, *The Illusion of Life: Disney Animation*

In animation, creating the "illusion of life" boils down not to mannerisms and naturalistic movement but to emotion. The audience empathizes with emotion. Actors are athletes of the heart. If Pluto gets a sheet of flypaper stuck on his nose (as he does in the 1934 animation *Playful Pluto*), the audience laughs because of how Pluto feels about it, his frustration as he tries to get it off. Flypaper on a nose is nothing more than an interesting fact if you remove emotion, right? When Pluto only succeeds in shifting the flypaper from one body part to another, he becomes increasingly frustrated; the more excited he gets, the harder he tries to free himself from the flypaper, and the funnier the scene becomes. Emotion builds, laughter builds.

Sociologists and medical and psychiatric experts agree that humans universally express six basic emotions: happiness, surprise, fear, anger, disgust, and sadness. The expression of contempt comes in a close seventh. There is disagreement, however, about whether facial expression is in fact a reflection of inner emotional states or whether it is a social "display." I read in *Psychology Today* that the human face has precisely forty-four muscles, and we are capable of making approximately five thousand facial expressions (Blum 1998, 32). I don't want to get too arcane here, but since animators traffic in facial expression, this subject is worth pursuing for a moment. Paul Ekman (1983), professor of psychology at the University of California in San Francisco, conducted some fascinating experiments in which he instructed acting students to assume facial poses. They were given no acting context at all, and with the students not even knowing what they were doing ("Raise your eyebrows very high. Now drop your jaw . . ."), he discovered that the poses themselves caused body temperature to fluctuate, blood pressure to rise or fall, and heart rate to vary. This essentially reversed the cause-and-effect of emotion and impulse as traditionally practiced by actors. Actors find the motivation that leads to action and emotion. But Ekman proved that it works the other way around, too. If you make a particular kind of face, it will cause you to feel certain emotions. Wild, isn't it? Emotion seems to be a two-way street and, since Ekman's experiments, similar exercises are included in some acting training. The bottom line is that emotion affects the way you move externally—and how you move externally affects the way you feel.

While it may be true that there are six or seven basic emotions and five thousand facial expressions, humans are more complex than that. Most of our expressions are mixtures, or hybrids. We easily send mixed messages. Professor Ekman has identified nineteen different versions of the smile, for example. Lovers exchange one kind of smile, and the smile exchanged between customers at the bank is another kind. Cultural influences can also alter the way emotions are expressed. European Americans tend to express public emotion differently than Asians, and a child who has been raised in a dysfunctional household will frequently send confusing emotional signals.

Animation has not arrived at the point where facial expressions could be, say, programmed into 3-D software for later retrieval. I take that back. They *could* be, but they would be gross generalities and would not be useful in a sophisticated feature film. Animators still are artists more than they are technicians, and the art requires more than selecting generic expressions of emotion.

Thinking that is not expressed as emotion or movement is basically a big zero, a nonevent, mere potential energy. Theatrically speaking, emotion is the goal—that is the essential element of acting, the point of empathy with the audience. When Wile E. Coyote is chasing Road Runner for the umpteenth time, he is driven by emotion. If he stopped to think about it, he'd probably give up the chase because it surely must be clear by now that he is not ever going to catch that bird. We in the audience empathize with his campaign, however, because we have all, at one time or another, been obsessed with something or someone.

Specific—as opposed to universal—situations and emotions are what create a response, a sense of empathy, in your audience. For example, the general fact that all humans die does not produce a feeling of grief in most of us. But the fact that your best friend has died *does* produce grief. So, if a playwright or a screenwriter wants to make a statement about the folly of always living for tomorrow, he will create a character that lives that way. When the character faces death and realizes she has missed the sweetness of life by not living fully in the moment, the audience feels her loss and regret. You see? The circuit begins with a general principle, or theme, and works backward to the specific—and the specific moment is the point of contact with the audience. (Whew! And you thought this book was just going to explain why Woody Woodpecker is crazy!) The drama (and comedy) is unique this way, functioning opposite of the way, say, most painters work. A painter will paint an image of something specific—a single sunflower, a setting sun, a Mona Lisa—and the viewer forms his own opinion about whatever universal principle may be suggested.

Empathy is not just something we talk about in acting. It is fundamental to human existence. It is evolutionary. Mothers empathize with their babies, which is how they know to pick them up when they cry. If you're standing in the kitchen with your husband when he is cooking dinner, and he slices his finger with a paring knife, you wince along with him because you identify with—empathize with—his emotional reaction to the injury. A psychologically healthy person is an empathic person. A sociopath is notably lacking in the empathy department. If he were empathic, he wouldn't be able to slit someone's throat and then go out for a burger.

President Bill Clinton made a political virtue out of being empathic when he told the voters, "I feel your pain." When King Kong sadly realizes that he can't get out of the cage, the audience empathizes with his feelings of fear and sadness; when the dwarfs cry around Snow White's death bed, we empathize with their grief; when someone wins an Academy Award, the TV-watching audience empathizes with the winner's gleeful feelings.

The audience empathizes with emotion, so finding points of empathy is the animator's key to theatrical success.

Charlie Chaplin and Empathy

I thought of the Tramp as a sort of Pierrot. With this conception I was freer to express and embellish the comedy with touches of sentiment.

—Charlie Chaplin

All great cartoon characters are based on human behavior we recognize in ourselves.

—Chuck Jones in *Chuck Amuck*

Charlie Chaplin brought empathy to comedy. His brilliance and innovation as a performer made him the first international movie star, and his influence on the world of comics and animation is huge. Cartoonist Pat Sullivan, for example, borrowed from Chaplin when he was drawing the *Sammy Johnsin* comic strip back in 1917. And later Sullivan and Otto Messmer produced a Little Tramp comic strip that was wildly popular. When Messmer moved from comic strips to animated films, many people considered his Felix the Cat character to be a knock-off of Charlie Chaplin.

But it was Walt Disney who got the most mileage out of Chaplin. He and Disney's resident art teacher Don Graham made sure that the Disney animators at the old Hyperion Boulevard studios in Los Angeles studied Chaplin movies frame by frame. Graham and the animators would do "action analysis" on them, studying the dynamics of Chaplin's movement and watching how he set up his gags. To be sure, they also studied Buster Keaton, Laurel and Hardy, and the other silent film stars, too, but it was Chaplin who was the most influential by a good distance.

What made this little man so popular and important? Some folks argue that it was his funny walk, the big shoes, the cane he twirled, his mustache. Yes, all of those things are funny, and they may have contributed to Chaplin as an endearing personality, but it was his ability to inspire empathy that was his true genius. Chaplin understood how to play to the heart, how to evoke laughter one moment and tears the next. Since he was targeting an international audience in a time before the talkies, he continually searched for the things that all humans have in common, the things that make us laugh and cry. Chaplin understood that audiences empathize with feelings, not thoughts or gags, and he looked for ways to allow the feelings of the Little Tramp to be visible. The important thing was not what happened to the Tramp, but how he *felt* about what had happened to him.

Empathy and *sympathy* are not interchangeable nouns. Psychologist Edward Tichener coined the word *empathy* in the early part of the twentieth century. It is akin to a German word, *Einfühlung*, which literally means "feeling into." The German word had been brought into use around 1907 by art critic Theodore Lipps when he was searching for a way to describe a mode of aesthetic perception. A person could "feel into" a painting, for instance. *Sympathy*, which means "feeling for," does not capture the same meaning as *empathy*. If you feel pity or concern for another person, that's sympathy. Empathy means that you identify with, and share in, the other person's feelings.

If an audience merely feels sorry for the character, the scene will fall flat. When a viewer empathizes with the character on screen, he is seeing his own potential to behave as that character is behaving. He *identifies* with the character. Empathy is based on the fact that we all act to survive, to live. Doesn't matter which culture or country, we start breathing at birth, and we keep trying to breathe until the last moment of our lives. Sounds simplistic, but it is actually a very profound truth for animators to recognize. In order for acting to rise to the level of art, it must inspire empathy (Bertolt Brecht's theories respectfully excepted, because they are not relevant to animation). This was the difference between Sennett's Keystone Kops and Chaplin's work as the Little Tramp in *The Gold Rush*. In the Keystone Kops series, there was no script, no plot to speak of, and the gags involved chase scenes and pratfalls. Pure slapstick comedy. A Kop would get his foot caught in a bucket and try to shake it off, kicking around wildly. That was the kind of comedy that was popular when Charlie Chaplin arrived in America. When the Little Tramp got his foot caught in the same bucket, he too tried to shake it off—but he would look around to see if anybody noticed his predicament! He was embarrassed by it. Immediately, the audience would empathize because we have all gotten our foot caught in the figurative bucket at one time or another. When the Keystone Kops did it, the audience laughed *at* the Kop; when Charlie did it, they laughed *with* him.

I'll wager that you have had many Chaplinesque moments in your life and didn't even realize it. I'll tell you about one of mine. When I first moved to sunny Los Angeles from chilly New York in 1976, I decided to go to the beach. Parking being a big problem in Santa Monica, I drove north along the Coast Highway until I found a grocery store with a large parking lot on the east side of the highway. Leaving my car in the lot, I made my way in a westerly direction, climbing through the broken chain-link fence. I walked along a winding out-of-the-way foot path, which doubled me back under the highway and deposited me onto a small and lovely beach not too far north of the ultra-rich Malibu Colony. After laying out my blanket on the sand, setting the portable radio dial to the golden-oldies station, and lathering on the suntan lotion, I glanced around at the people on the beach, pleased with myself for having settled in like a local. That was when I noticed the two of them: a handsome young man and woman, just emerging from the ocean, stark naked. Focusing more closely, I shifted my view slightly to my right to see if anybody else noticed Venus and Adonis. Several more bare bottoms shone in the sunshine. I looked to my left, same thing. Then it dawned on me that some of the folks were starting to look at *me* with annoyed expressions on their faces! I casually checked my watch, considered for a moment the nonexistent appointment I had forgotten about, gathered my blanket and accoutrements, and, as if I passed this way every Sunday, walked slowly back to the path that had led me to what was obviously a clothing-optional beach. On the way back to the car, I imagined the scene I had just been part of as it might have been played in a comedy movie. The actor playing my part would have gawked at the nudity, his jaw dropping with incredulity. But that would have been cheap movie making. In real life, I had personified a Chaplin moment. My first impulse was not to gawk (though I surely was gawking inside . . .), but to look around to see if anybody else realized there were naked people on the beach. In other words, I didn't play the moment for laughs, but for the humanity, which made it really funny.

Charlie Chaplin's Little Tramp character was just that, a tramp, a drifter. Chuck Jones says he knows of no lasting comedian who was not a loser, and he cites Chaplin as an example. I understand his point, because the Tramp rarely had more than a few coins in his pocket, and he was never very far from starving, but I disagree about the loser part.

There is a major difference between being a victim and being victimized. The Little Tramp was no victim. He was a survivor who was frequently victimized. No matter how dismal the circumstances of his life were, no matter how hungry or cold he was, he never gave up, and he never lost his self-respect. There was pathos to the Little Tramp, yet he did not want to be pitied. If he had given up, if he indeed were a loser, the unspoken audience reaction would be, in effect, "That Little Tramp sure is a sad character. I hope he can get his act together. I, on the other hand, would never give up." In other words, the audience would *sympathize* with the Little Tramp, but if he gave up the good fight, they would not *empathize*. This is, in my opinion, one of the major differences between the comedy of Buster Keaton and that of Charlie Chaplin. Keaton frequently drew sympathy with his expressionless reactions and hangdog demeanor. In a BBC television documentary about his life and achievements, Keaton said that he never *tried* to make audiences feel sorry for him, but "if they did, that was okay." I am convinced that this is the reason Keaton occupies a slightly lesser position in cinematic history than Chaplin does. He was a brilliant clown and mime, but he was uneducated and unsophisticated about the actor/audience contract and about empathy. Walt Disney had an innate understanding of empathy, which was why I think he identified with Chaplin so much.

Charlie Chaplin never used the actual word *empathy*, but he had a solid grasp of the empathic process. He just knew. He was brilliant. In *The Adventurer*, for example, he included a gag in which he spilled an ice cream cone down the dress of this upper-class matron. Explaining the psychology behind the gag some years later, he said,

> there were two real points of human nature involved in it. One was the delight the average person takes in seeing wealth and luxury in trouble. (It would not have been funny for the ice cream to have fallen on a poor woman.) The other was the tendency of the human being to experience within himself the emotions he sees on the stage or screen. (Robinson 1985, 202)

That's empathy.

This is the great acting lesson for all actors and animators: Go for the empathy as much as the gag. Remember the heart. Don't just try to be funny. Evoke tears as well as laughter.

All of acting rests on the search for the positive motivation, the survival mechanism, in the characters. As Walter Kerr once observed, "The secret of Chaplin, as a character, is that he can be anyone" (1975, cover). No matter what the awful circumstance, Chaplin's character always hung on to a basic respect for the human race. He was serious and funny, both at the same time. "All of my pictures are built around the idea of getting me into trouble and so giving me the chance to be desperately serious in my attempt to appear as a normal little gentleman," he wrote early in his Hollywood career, adding: "That is why, no matter how desperate the predicament is, I am always very much in earnest about clutching my cane, straightening my derby hat, and fixing my tie, even though I have just landed on my head."

Now, apply the empathy litmus test to your favorite cartoon characters like, say, Bugs Bunny or Sylvester the Cat and see if they are not cockeyed optimists, too. Chuck Jones acknowledges that Bugs' optimism is a key element in the rabbit's character, and I'm surprised he didn't recognize Bugs' roots in Charlie Chaplin's work. As the old saying goes, Everybody loves a winner. It started with Chaplin. Pop some corn, put your feet up, and study him hard.

A Process of Exposing, Not Hiding

Here is another of those tricky distinctions between actors and animators: When creating a character, an actor tends to work from the inside out; animators, by contrast, tend to work from the outside in. Actors think of exposing themselves through the character. When acting is right, it feels mildly embarrassing, like you are taking off your clothes in front of strangers. The animator doesn't work like that because he doesn't work in the fleeting moment. But this is important: The fact that actors expose themselves is what makes each actor's perspective unique.

While it is true that the audience sees a finished and well-developed character on stage when the curtain goes up, the actor who created the character does not experience the process of acting as hiding, or becoming another person. To him, it feels like truth telling. From an actor's perspective, the goal is to merge his own honest impulses with those of the character he is playing. I'm not suggesting that the actor tries to make each of his characters behave like the actor does in real life. No, the challenge for the actor is to identify what the character is doing in the scene, and then to find in himself the impulse that will lead to that action.

A process of exposing, not hiding

Actors do not become characters they play. You can't, in reality, be anybody other than yourself, right? You can't be me, and I can't be you, and neither one of us can be Hamlet. But we both understand vengeance in our own ways, and therein lies the secret of how you and I can both play Hamlet. Our performances would be similar in that we both say Shakespeare's lines, but what you think makes Hamlet tick is different from what I think makes Hamlet tick. We each look at life in our own unique way.

The fun in acting is to play characters that are different from yourself because, when you do, you are telling an audience what it is that you understand about this character. This is how acting rises above the Mickey Rooney, "Hey, kids, let's put on a show!" level and becomes art. At its artistic best, all acting is character acting. But we as actors don't so much "create" the character as we "release" the character. Michelangelo spoke of exposing the hidden figure within the marble rather than creating a figure. So it is with actors and their characters.

We have the potential to be anything in life. If you had been born into less money or more money, or if you had lost a foot in a motorcycle accident when you were sixteen, your life would be quite different today. If your mother had died in childbirth, you'll never know how her influence on you might have affected your ultimate maturity. We are all born a blank slate. Given your genetic parameters, circumstances in your life are what mold you. It is possible that, given different circumstances in your life, you might have turned out to be an U.S. senator, a doctor, or a clown at Ringling Brothers. You could be in jail or in a monastery or on the moon.

In our own lives, we emphasize the character traits that get us the most mileage, the most success. One person's demeanor may be that of the jokester, another takes the quiet, studious approach. Yet another is a born politician. There is a good chance that the quiet studious person got that way partly because nobody ever laughed at her jokes much anyway. The jokester, by contrast, gets plenty of positive feedback for his gregarious ways. When you are acting, you find the parts in yourself that would be like the character you are playing, and you hoist those up the flagpole, allowing them to be more powerful than your regular street personality.

Peter Brook put it best: "Preparing a character is the opposite of building—it is demolishing, removing brick by brick everything in the actor's muscles, ideas, and inhibitions that stands between him and the part" (1987, 7). When an experienced actor is cast in a role, he immediately tries to find the potential in himself that would cause him to behave the way the character in the story is called on to behave. Acting is a process of identifying with and exposing, not of hiding, and it works in the first person, not the third-person reference.

The character is I, not *he* or *she*. You find the potential in yourself to behave like the character, and then you tell the truth about it. If, for example, a heterosexual actor were cast in the film biography of Oscar Wilde, it would not be helpful for him to say, "Well, personally, I would never do homosexual things as Mr. Wile did." It's more constructive to acknowledge that we all have the potential to behave in all sorts of different ways, and then to get on with it. He would study the play, learn about the character, and try to find points of empathy, a conjunction between himself and that character. If he were cast to play Stanley Kowalski, for example, he would try to find the part of himself that expresses himself physically. Stanley is not a man who is good with words. In a moment of frustration, he is more likely to wipe the dishes off the table, sending them flying into the wall, than he is to talk things out in the family counselor's office.

The animator similarly tells the truth. If the character you are animating needs to be the most beautiful, most handsome, or most powerful person in the world (Kent Mansley in *The Iron Giant*, the queen in *Snow White*, Jafar in *Aladdin*), you have to identify with that personality trait before you can bring the character believably to life. If you deny your own potential to be an obnoxious and/or dangerous overachiever, then you're not going to get very far creatively with that character.

Adrenaline Moments

One of the most instructive aspects of Shakespeare's plays is how important every scene is. If the guy doesn't get the girl, France falls! If Romeo can't have Juliet, he'd rather be dead. Shylock doesn't simply want interest on his loan; he wants a pound of Antonio's flesh. After reading a 1996 medical study about the function of adrenaline in peak moments, I have come to think of scenes in movies and plays as *adrenaline moments*. I ask myself if this is a moment that the characters will remember when they are in old age. "Yep, I 'member the day I broke up with Rose. Boy, she shore wuz pretty. . . ." or "That Wile E. Coyote almost got me that one day, out by the cliffs. I remember it well. . . ."

I blame television programming—which generally plays to the lowest common denominator and functions as a vehicle for delivering good-humored consumers to the commercials—for trivializing human relations in contemporary culture. And since

Adrenaline moments

culture is mirrored in the arts, relationships in movies and plays have also been trivialized. The public has been anesthetized, numbed by the "vast wasteland" television programming has become (read Newton Minow [Minow and Lamay 1996]).

If you want to truly captivate your audience, remember this: They aren't interested in seeing another run-of-the-mill boyfriend/girlfriend story. They want to see Romeo and Juliet, Anthony and Cleopatra. Peter Brook, the famous Shakespearean director, gives an important lesson to actors when he advises that, "no matter how much you feel, your character feels more. No matter how much you love, your character loves more" (Brook 1995).

A movie is a dream. It is a sequence of important moments, strung together, telling a story. Every scene, every conversation, every point of view carries significance. Consider this: A movie can only be just so long, right? Make a movie that runs three hours, and the exhibitors growl. An hour and a half or so is just about it, right? Well, if you are limited to an hour and a half, then you can only include x number of images, pictures. You have to select from all the possibilities in the world, in the service of your story.

A person will always remember where he or she was the first time he made love, where he was and how he felt when his wife left him, how he felt the day he came across a hungry coyote in a clearing in the woods. If you are old enough, you remember where you were the day John F. Kennedy was assassinated. You remember where you were when your parent died, when your child was born. What we know now is that, when an important event happens in our life, we "mark" it with adrenaline. Our brain is literally washed with adrenaline, sending the message: "Remember this. It's important." Presumably this is because, when we were more primitive humans, we needed to know what dangerous situations to avoid. First time we were attacked by a saber-toothed tiger, adrenaline helped us learn to avoid that kind of animal in the future.

Heroes and Villians

The queen in *Snow White* had to be cold, ruthless, mean, and dramatic. Nothing would be gained by developing her personality any further or by letting the audience discover her weaknesses. Like a Shakespearean monarch, she had to be regal and beyond the reach of common people.

—Frank Thomas and Ollie Johnston, *The Illusion of Life: Disney Animation*

Frank Thomas and Ollie Johnston speak at length about the making of Disney villains in their book named, appropriately enough, *The Disney Villain* (1993). They are explicit in their insistence that the villain must be bigger than life and have no regrets. It seems to me that this might be a workable formula for a classic fairy tale, which is what *Snow White and the Seven Dwarfs* is, but animation today is sailing past the fairy tale stage, taking its place in the mainstream of adult entertainment. Fairy tales don't traffic in subtleties. They require an archetypal hero and villain and a moral conclusion—and that's it. When it comes to the heroes and villains of the twenty-first century, however, we need to create more nuanced characters.

Consider for a moment the Disney animated version of *The Hunchback of Notre Dame*. It appears to me that the story's villain, Claude Frollo, was created in the mode of the queen in *Snow White*—a one-dimensional baddie—and I'm guessing this is a formula that can be traced back to the reasoning of the Grand Old Men. Frollo is, in my opinion, dastardly from first entrance to final exit, the kind of character who literally would kick babies down the stairs. Following the logic from the 1930s and 1940s, I can see where the creators figured this would be frightening—but Victor Hugo's *Hunchback of Notre Dame* is decidedly not a fairy tale. It wouldn't have taken much to flesh out Claude Frollo's character a bit more, and I contend it would have made for a better movie. Let's first try to come up with workable definitions for *hero* and *villain*.

To me, a hero is an ordinary person who has to rise to extraordinary heights to fight an extraordinary villain or situation. Alfred Hitchcock made a hero out of Cary Grant in *North by Northwest*. Gary Cooper was certainly a hero in *High Noon*, a workaday sheriff who has to defend an entire town single-handedly. Jimmy Stewart was a hero in *Mr. Smith Goes to Washington*, fighting political corruption, the biggest and ugliest enemy of all. And while a passerby who pulls victims out of a burning car wreck is a hero, the parent who jumps in front of a car to protect his own child is not. A naturally talented athlete is not a hero, even if he climbs Mount Everest, but an athlete who overcomes a diagnosis of terminal cancer to win the Tour de France, as Lance Armstrong did in 1999, is a hero in my book. Those who smuggled Jews out of Germany during WWII were heroes, but an Army general is not a hero just because he is a general. And, yes, Quasimodo—hunchback, bad eye, and all—would fit my definition of a hero. Despite his unusual abode in the cathedral and the cruel circumstances of his upbringing, he is basically an ordinary kind of person who longs to be just one of the gang.

A villain, by contrast, is an ordinary person who has a fatal flaw, a blind spot in his psychology, something that torments him and causes obsession. Captain Nemo in *20,000 Leagues Under the Sea* is a great villain. Adolph Hitler was a villain. Captain Ahab in *Moby-Dick* is a great villain. One of my favorite cinematic villains is Cruella De Vil in *101 Dalmations.* She's a regular enough lady, but she has this flaw that causes her to obsess about owning a puppy-skin coat. Hannibal Lecter in *Silence of the Lambs* and its sequel is the very definition of an excellent movie villain—a medical doctor run amuck, morphed into a serial killer who—gasp!—cannibalizes his victims! You don't get much more awful than that, now do you?

Okay, now that we know what heroes and villains are, let's talk about what to do with them acting-wise. The key once again, still, and always is empathy.

An actor's job is to create in the audience a sense of empathy, and this is true whether the character is a hero or a villain. If I were cast to portray Hitler, I would try to find in myself the potential to do what he did. Hitler didn't think he was evil or a villain. He figured the world had a Jewish problem and needed what Germany had to offer as a solution. As ugly as that may be, I—as an actor—must justify such behavior. It does me no good at all to deny that I have the potential to carry out mass executions. If, after my performance as Hitler, members of the audience say to themselves, "My God, I understand the man! I can see how this terrible thing happened and could happen again!"—then I am a success. If they say on the way out, "Yep, that Hitler was an evil fellow, alright. Good thing he's dead, God and the U.S.A. prevailed, and we don't have to worry about people like him any more"—then I have failed. The point of art is to say something about life, about living. It's not about preaching to the choir.

Whenever I hear an actor in one of my classes say that she cannot relate to the character she is playing, I stop the class cold. It is virtually impossible to give a compelling performance if you cannot relate to your character.

When Anthony Hopkins portrayed Hannibal Lector, he had people in the audience actually rooting for the cannibal. You know why? Go back and watch the movie again and you'll see that Hopkins allowed in these little slivers of humanity. In the scene where Jodi Foster stands outside his cage and tells him about how her father met his violent death, you can see in Hopkins' nonverbal reactions that he is (1) stimulated by her description of death, and (2) empathizing with her feelings of loss. It's the second part that makes

Hopkins' work so wonderful. He makes us identify with the man. We all can identify with the emotions of a person who has lost a loved one. Brilliant acting.

Now let's return to Frollo's character development. There is a lot to admire about Disney's version of *The Hunchback of Notre Dame*, not the least of which are the gorgeous Paris backgrounds and the catchy show tunes. And it was to be expected that Disney would convert pathetic, stone-deaf, silently furious Quasimodo into a sort of good-natured chipmunk of a fellow with a back problem and one cute eye. But a fundamental error was made in the design of the villain, Claude Frollo and, in my opinion, this factor more than any other robs the movie of the greatness it might have otherwise achieved.

In this movie, we lose any sense of humanity in Frollo. We never even hear about how he cared for his younger brother after their parents died, or why he was moved to protect and raise Quasimodo in the first place. Indeed, in the movie, his first reaction to the idea of adopting the child is to protest. "What?! I'm to be saddled with this misshapen . . ."

From beginning to end, the animated Frollo is unempathic. There is no way for an audience to identify with him—and he therefore loses some of his power to frighten. The thing that is scariest is the recognition of the villain in each of us. Victor Hugo gave us that option in his book; Disney did not.

It would not have taken much to do for Frollo what Hopkins did for Hannibal Lecter. A single scene in which he could experience amusement, a touch of human kindness, would have done the trick. Those figurines that Quasimodo carved in his living quarters presented an opportunity. It appears that the only reason for them to be in the movie was to set up the commercial tie-ins. But suppose Quasimodo was carving the delicate figures to please Frollo? Suppose Frollo was truly charmed by them? A moment of gentleness perhaps? Suppose Frollo were charmed and then, as a reaction against his own weakness, he swept the figurines off onto the floor! That would have created a point of empathy. A warm connection between Frollo and Quasimodo, however fleeting, would have made the later terror in the movie much more frightening. Heck, it would have been nice if Frollo had even liked his horse! When he tumbles from the cathedral at the end of the movie, we are supposed to be happy that there are no more Claude Frollos among us. The one who existed has bitten the dust. To me, that is not getting the most mileage for the villainous buck.

It is true that, in order to have a strong hero, you have to have an even stronger villain. The stakes have to be huge in order to make the fight worthwhile in cinematic and theatrical terms—and to carry a theme.

If *Snow White and the Seven Dwarfs* were farce, I would agree with Thomas and Johnston when they say that there would have been no gain in deepening the character of the queen. Maybe they're right, and we'll never know for sure, but in general I contend that you cannot go wrong by making your villains empathic. True, it is frightening to have a big train bearing down on you, but it is more frightening to know that a sociopath who demonstrates the occasional empathic trait is at the controls.

Movement and Body Language
5

Animation *is* movement. Movement *is* animation. What a person in the audience sees creates a much stronger impression than what he hears. In fact, if you want to prioritize the senses, they would rank this way:

1.   Sight: We see something before we can hear it.

2.   Hearing: We hear something before we can smell it.

3.   Smell: We smell something before we can touch it.

4.   Touch: We touch something before we can taste it.

5.   Taste: Taste is intimate, as close as we can get.

A character's body language is going to transmit a more powerful message than his dialogue. Politicians and Madison Avenue ad execs understand this better than anybody, which explains all those flag-waving, sappy campaign ads that saturate the airwaves every four years. It doesn't really matter what sort of awful lies they are telling, just as long as they're kissing babies and standing in front of a flag. Anthropologist Edward T. Hall says in his book *The Hidden Dimension*, "it is probable that the eyes may be as much as a thousand times as effective as the ears in sweeping up information" (Hall 1969, 42). The evolutionary reason for this is that when we were still running around on the savannahs, hiding from saber-toothed tigers, we had to be able to detect predators before they were close enough to eat us. If we had to wait until we could hear or smell them, we'd be lunch.

For proof of the power of visuals, consider how long it takes for you to form an impression about the people that you see on the street. I am writing this paragraph while sitting in the window of my favorite Italian coffee shop in downtown Palo Alto, California, on a sunny October afternoon. A steady stream of cars and pedestrians is passing by on University Avenue outside, but street noise is isolated from me. All I can hear is the music on the store music system and the happy chatter of a few patrons. The fact that I can't hear outside noises, however, doesn't stop me from forming conclusions about what I am seeing. There is a man sitting directly across the street from me, for instance. He is under a tree in front of the bank; he has freshly barbered blonde hair, is beardless, and is in a wheelchair; he just finished drinking what appears to be a milkshake or soda from a large Dixie cup. He is lighting his cigarette with a lighter, not a match; he is wearing a loosely fitting burgundy T-shirt and black slacks; his left foot is propped up on the frame of the well-traveled chair, causing his left knee to jut higher above his lap than his right. That suggests to me that he is not paralyzed from the waist down. He's maybe thirty years old and appears to be in good general health except for not being able to walk. He looks brighter than the average bear, probably has at least a high school education and, this being mid-afternoon on a weekday, is probably unemployed. The fact that he lit his cigarette with a lighter says to me that he is a regular smoker and may have an obstinate attitude. Everybody knows smoking is a health hazard, so why would a person who is already in a wheelchair be smoking? I figure he probably is the sort who will not let anybody tell him what to do. Smoking is a sign of his independence.

Now the truth is that I have no basis on which to conclude these things about that man. I don't know why he is in that wheelchair or, in fact, anything at all about him. It is unfair for me to be forming any conclusions, yet I do it. You, too, form continual and immediate impressions based on what you see—and more relevant to the topic under discussion, so does every member of every theatre and movie audience in the world. The visual impression created on stage or screen is more important than the spoken word. This is why I am firmly convinced that strong animation can save a weak voice-actor performance, but the strongest voice performance cannot save weak animation. (I'm frequently annoyed by reviews of animated features because too many reviewers credit the voice-actors with the success of the final film, treating the animation almost as an incidental element!)

Of course, I'm not suggesting that visuals and sound are an either/or proposition. Both music and sound effects accompany movies. The music frequently creates a mood that vastly enhances the visuals. The Gary Cooper movie *High Noon* is a good example. In its prerelease edited form, the haunting theme song, "Do Not Forsake Me, Oh My Darlin'" was not included. Studio execs decided the movie didn't work and insisted that the track be added. I defy you to imagine that movie without the song. It makes the movie!

This fact of life about vision versus hearing is an appropriate introduction to the general topic of movement. Movement does not exist in a vacuum. Your arms, and the dog's legs, don't just flail around senselessly. Movement is a result of thinking and emotion. An animator really should have a profound understanding of the connections between thoughts and movement, emotion and movement, how movement impacts on the audience and how it impacts on other actors in the scene.

Body Language

When I began work on this book, I asked several animators what they would like to see in a book on the subject of acting for animators. How could I be most helpful? All but one suggested prominently that I include an encyclopedia of physiological movement—descriptions of movement that makes a character appear happy, anxious, sad, and angry. I'm including a miniguide to generalized movement, but I do it with some reservations because good performance animation cannot be codified that way. Acting is not like a Chinese menu, where you take this facial expression from column A and that leg movement from column B. There are as many different body movements and facial expressions as there are characters. Each character is unique and has his own identity.

Suppose the character you are animating has a cold and you have to make her sneeze. How would you specify the action involved in a sneeze? Look under S in a book of facial expressions? You'd discover a garden variety "Achoo!!" But I know a woman who, when she sneezes, holds her nose and squeaks, evidently running the risk that she'll blow out her eardrums. By contrast, when I sneeze, it's so loud my wife says that I scare the dog. My point is that there is not a generic sneeze, or a generic nose blow, any more than there is a generic way to scratch a mosquito bite. While it is true that these sorts of details will help bring a character to life, it is also true that nuance—and real "illusion of life"—resides in the *way* the details are drawn. And the *way* details are drawn has everything to do with the artist's perceptions of and attitudes about the world around him, coupled with his understanding of his character's value structure, physical attributes, and situational context.

Well-trained actors spend at least some of their time in dance studios. Having been an actor myself for thirty years, I have studied dance, mime, and Laban Movement Theory (discussed later in this chapter). But, as an actor, I can tell you that we do not think about movement the way animators do. I recommend a wonderful book entitled *The Inner Game of Tennis* (1974), written by W. Timothy Gallwey. Gallwey says that if you want to play championship tennis, you need to stop thinking about your movement and your serve, and start thinking about where you want the ball to be. So yes, by all means, train well. But then, to move on to the next step, trust the training and focus on your intention. That's the way actors consider movement. It's something you need to be able to do well, but it's not something you think about a lot.

The mechanics of movement, important as that may be to animators, are second nature to actors. Actors learn to *allow* physical expression, not to *cause* it. It is actually an internal thing, not external. Internal impulses (thinking) are expressed externally, always through the body, sometimes through words. Try acting in a scene in which you move nothing but your face and see how far you get. Movement precedes words, but it is also true that, from an actor's perspective, if you are thinking about how you are moving, you will not be pursuing your objectives in the scene; you won't fully be playing your action. It's like when you ride a bike, you don't think about your feet pushing the pedals.

I have come to the conclusion that many animators have a misconception about how actors deal with movement. Preston Blair, for example, contends in *How to Animate Film Cartoons* that "The actor learns the craft—how to always walk or move with a meaning—to never pause unless you have a reason for it—when you pause, pause as long as you can. . . . Hold a gesture as long as possible to let it register and sink in" (Blair 1990, 14). With due respect to Mr. Blair, I know of nothing in the actor's lexicon about pausing for as long as you can. There is a rule of acting that says you ought not to move without a reason, without motivation, but that's it. The purpose of movement is destination. There's nothing in there about pausing as long as you can, but I understand that pauses take on physical properties for the animator. As my animator friend Doug Aberle observes, "Watch sometimes how long Daffy Duck may stare at the camera after being shot, before his face falls off." BIG pause! In general, however, sometimes you pause, and sometimes you don't. Depends on the moment and your objectives and, most often, an actor is as surprised as everybody else when he pauses on stage.

Walt Disney discovered that character expression works best when it involves the whole body, not just the face. Movement begins in the area of your navel and radiates outward into your limbs. Ask ten people what the most expressive part of their body is, and nine of them will tell you it's the face. The truth is that our hands and arms are the most expressive parts of our bodies. When you think of your body as a form, a block that is filling space, you see that the head and face occupy a tiny part of the form. This lesson is hard for many new actors to grasp, coming as they do from the world of cinema where they are raised on the extreme facial close-up. "It's all in the eyes" is the maxim you hear all the time when you first learn about movie acting. It all comes down to close-ups, and close-ups are about eyes. But that's no place to hang your hat if you are trying to understand human psychology and expression. This is why animators who rely too heavily on that mirror on the desk to work out facial expressions are doing only half the work. It is true that actors and animators must be masters of portraying emotion, but you do yourself a disservice if you believe that emotion is mainly expressed by the face. There was a famous review of Geraldine Page's Broadway performance in a Tennessee Williams play (*Summer and Smoke*, I think), in which the reviewer observed that "Miss Page does more acting with her back than most actors do with their fronts." So did Charlie Chaplin. And so it is—or should be—with animation. Get the body first, and *then* worry about the face.

When I was seventeen years old, I saw my first performance of *The Dark of the Moon* at Arena Stage in Washington, D.C. Rene Auberjonois played the witch boy who falls in love with Barbara Allen, the human girl. He makes a deal with the head witch that allows him to become human on a trial basis. Now, the way most productions of this play deal with the transition from witch to human is with wild costumes. When the witch boy is a witch, he may have twigs growing out of his back for instance. And when he becomes human, the twigs are removed. Well, Rene Auberjonois did something in that show that made a dramatic impression on me as an actor and testifies to the power of visuals in human movement. He chose to move close to the ground when he was a witch, slinking around like a weasel, on all fours. After he made the deal with the head witch, he played subsequent scenes in increasingly erect postures. I recall that, at one point, he was tilted from the waist at about a forty-five-degree angle. Then, when he made his first entrance as a full human being, he walked out onto the stage standing fully erect, proud and tall. I get chills just thinking about it even now, almost forty years later! It was as if the lights in the theatre had gotten brighter. The actor had mimicked the evolution of man, from muck to full power. The words of the play were the same as I have now learned they are in every production. It was what that marvelous actor did with the physical movement that made the impression.

A person's physical movement is a compensation for, or reaction to, whatever is going on with him physically or psychically. Here's an example: I have an acting student in my San Francisco class who suffers from slipped discs in her spine. Invariably, she arrives at class late, walking slowly, and when she enters, she brings with her a pillow to sit on. Another student is a dancer, and I don't recall him ever sitting on a chair or sofa in the regular way. He prefers to sit cross-legged on the floor, back erect. Or, if he sits on a sofa, he'll manage to position himself in a stretching pose. Mind you, none of this is done for effect. It's just the way he handles his body. Rene Auberjonois, in that play, decided that the power of the human was in the spine and in our evolutionary struggle to defy gravity.

With this proviso—that there really is not an ironclad, one-of-a-kind, checklist guide to physical movement—I offer the following generalities of body language for you to consider:

- Arms folded across the chest can indicate that the person is "closed," intractable. Hands clasped behind one's back or folded across one's crotch indicates low-status, literally signaling that "I won't defend myself."

- Confidence manifests itself as relaxation, and relaxation manifests itself in a feeling of weight, not lightness. A confident character has weight, centeredness.

- A cerebral person will tend to lead with his forehead. Film actors learn how to employ this fact of life. Notice how much more compelling and forceful an actor on screen seems when his gaze is first cast downward and then shifts upward, toward the camera. This would be in contrast in leading with your chin, exposing your throat. Remember Gomer Pyle, portrayed by Jim Nabors on television? His head was always up, throat exposed. Head down, shifting upward signifies a strategist; head up, throat exposed signifies a nonthreatening, often fun, kind of person. Significantly, young children lead with their heads up. That's because learning the strategies of life is an adult thing. If a young child were to cast his gaze downward and shift up toward the camera, the effect could be chilling.

- A man with a beer gut has a lot of pressure on his lower back. When he sits in a chair, he will tend to use his arms and hands to ease the descent, perhaps bracing himself on the arms of the chair.

- When a person in conversation is interrupted, he may first turn his shoulders in the direction of the interruption before he turns his head, so he can complete whatever he is saying.

- Embarrassment is a low-status emotion, a way of defusing a tense moment. When you are embarrassed, you tend to shrink in space. You cast your gaze downward, your hands tend to rise to at least partly cover your face. Usually, when a person is embarrassed, he is acknowledging a truth of some kind. A kid tosses a ball through the living room window, and he's embarrassed. He did a bad thing. You discover that your fly is unzipped in front of the church group, and you are embarrassed. The top of your bathing suit comes off when you dive in the pool, and the resulting applause from onlookers embarrasses you.

- Anxiety is a heady energy, concentrated above the chest line and into the head. Woody Allen, to cite a popular example, typically displays a high power center, with arms and hands gesticulating wildly. This is a result of his philosophy of life. Woody operates on the premise that death is probably going to come sooner rather than later, and it makes him nervous. Mahatma Ghandi, on the other hand, presumably also knew that we all die, but he was comfortable with the idea, and so displayed a lower power center and gracefulness.

- When body movements extend above the waist, above the shoulders, they are "light" in nature; body movements below the waist are more associated with "weight" or "heaviness." Gravity is pulling harder.

- As a person gets older, his spine settles, and the character begins to move in reaction to discomfort. When you see old people walking down the street with little mincing steps, it is because it would hurt them to take bigger steps. And note how very old people tend to keep their mouths open as they walk, perhaps to allow in more oxygen. When an elderly person turns to looks slightly behind him, he will turn his entire upper body, not just his neck. That's because of stiffness in the upper spine. I still remember my granddaddy, trying to back out of the driveway at his house in Atlanta. He shouldn't have been driving at all at his age, but back then they didn't seem to make as big a deal about it. In order to drive in reverse, he didn't even attempt to turn his body around to look directly out the back window. That hurt his neck too much. So he watched the reverse image in the rearview mirror as he accelerated carefully backward. That's not how they want you do to it at the DMV.

Power Centers

The notion of shifting power centers is a particularly useful tool for animators. The basic idea is that, when we stand and walk with ease, our power center is in our chest, leading us forward. Try it. Just get up and walk around the room in a relaxed fashion or, as I prefer to say, "with ease." Can you feel the power generating from your chest? Now, let the power center move into your stomach, dropping from your chest. A pregnant woman walks this way. Try moving the power center to your feet. Let it pull you along, shuffling. Suddenly, you feel like a street bum, a wino. Put the power center behind your neck and let it push you instead of pull you. Feel the energy accelerate? Put the power center six inches over your head and dangle from it, let it make you dance.

In 1996, Michael Keaton starred in an underrated movie entitled *Multiplicity*, in which he played a man who clones himself in order to make life easier. "Two of me is better than one of me" is the logic. The thing is that the clones, all played by Keaton, have very different personalities. One is a macho kind of guy, another is very politically correct and accommodating, and another is ultraweird and unpredictable, even zany. I recommend that you rent this movie and study what Keaton has accomplished, keeping in mind this business about power centers. The politically correct clone has a high power center, in his upper chest; the macho clone has a low power center, in his groin.

An anxious person has a power center in his head. Think of Woody Allen or the comedienne Joan Rivers. Did you ever see Woody Allen's movie, *Play It Again, Sam*? In it, Humphrey Bogart—à la *Casablanca*—appears in the Allen character's fantasy, instructing him on how to be a "real man," how to "get a dame." Allen's a nervous wreck, a man with very heady energy, a high power center; Bogart, a man's man, has a very low power center, is unflappable.

Next time you're at a loss with a character you're animating, try shifting the power center.

The Psychological Gesture

Words express an underlying gesture. There was a time in our evolution when we pointed and grunted to make ourselves understood. Then we developed speech and, gradually, words have taken the place of most gestures. Sometimes we combine words with gestures for special emphasis—like when we yell at the driver who just cut us off on the freeway—but most of the time we let our words do the talking while we make rather unspecific movements with our arms and hands.

Animators can make use of this observation in a couple of ways. First, you can animate a character by pretending he doesn't have words at his disposal. How would the character express himself if he only had the use of his body, hands, and arms? Second, you can enhance dialogue by adding specific gestures rather than general ones.

For example, the word *broken* in the sentence "My heart is broken" can be expressed by miming the breaking of a stick. Try this experiment: With your hands down by your side, say that line out loud. Did you do it? Well, go ahead and do it. This lesson won't mean much unless you do the work. Say, right out loud, "My heart is broken." Nobody's watching. Good. Now, make the gesture of breaking that stick of wood. Good. Now say the line again and do the gesture at the same time, breaking the wood precisely when you say the word *broken*. See how much stronger the line sounds, how

69

much stronger it feels? Now, put your hands in your pocket or down by your side, say the line out loud and *imagine* breaking that stick. Make the stick-breaking gesture internally. The line still sounds stronger, just as if you were actually, physically making the gesture with your hands out front. Amazing, huh?

Now let's take the notion of the psychological gesture a step further, incorporating "atmosphere." Imagine a car wreck on a highway. Police cars are in attendance, lights flashing in the drizzly early evening air. There is a yellow tarp covering what must be a body in one of the wrecked cars. A man is sitting on the curb, sobbing. Got the picture? Okay, now imagine that you arrive on the scene, on foot. Can you feel the "atmosphere" of the place? It's quite different from the atmosphere in the coffee shop down the street or the atmosphere at a playground. Notice how your body reacts to the very idea of atmosphere at that car wreck scene? Notice how you tense up? There is a valuable acting lesson there. There is an inherent atmosphere in every scene, every setting. Rather than simply entering a scene as if you (or your character) are all that exists in the world, let the atmosphere of the scene inform you emotionally. React to it, factor it into your actions. Let it color the intentions you bring into the scene. This principle is what makes haunted house scenarios so scary, by the way. The atmosphere is designed to scare the pants off you.

For further reading about the psychological gesture, pick up a copy of *On the Technique of Acting* by Michael Chekhov (1991). He's the fellow who first popularized the idea in acting theory.

Effect of Alcohol and Drugs on Movement

Alcohol and marijuana relax the muscles, causing the character to yield to the pull of gravity. A drunk character is heavy, and his movement is slower, the arcs more fluid. Cocaine will wire the character, causing him to resist the pull of gravity, and his movement will be swifter, the arcs quicker.

Acting-wise, you can lump all external substances, whether they stimulate or depress, together under this maxim: Allow the substance to do whatever that particular substance does to the body—and then act to control it, to hide it. If it relaxes you and slows you down, strive for alertness and muscle tension; if it wires you, like cocaine, strive to relax, to moderate your behavior.

A drunken person—unless he is *trying* to be drunk, like at a frat party or with a bunch of drunken sailors—will act against the loss of control. The person who drinks too much an at office parties, or on a date, circumstances where it is a liability to appear too out-of-control, are worth studying. Even as they are getting mentally and physically slower, they strive to appear alert, even erudite. It is a hallmark of the amateur actor that, when he plays a drunk, he stumbles and mumbles across the stage, really layering it on. For an accurate, dramatic live-action depiction of drunken behavior, watch the Jack Lemmon movie *The Days of Wine and Roses*. For a comedic live-action depiction, watch Dudley Moore's performance in *Arthur*.

Pantomime

Pantomime is one of those words that can lead to confusion because there is "English Pantomime," which involves fairy tales and cross-dressing, and there is the kind of pantomime for which Marcel Marceau is famous. The origins of both are unclear, but they evidently are rooted in Commedia dell'Arte in sixteenth-century Italy. The Harlequin character got into the act somewhere along the way, donning whiteface, to emphasize facial expression. Today, an informal man-on-the-street poll will surely show that most civilians consider pantomime to be a kind of wordless acting—something very distinct from the acting you see in movies. Consider this: An actor expresses love with words, sighs, and accompanying gestures. A mime generally does not speak at all, so he expresses love with poses, attitudes—maybe he will cross his hands across his heart and put a funny expression on his face.

The way the word *pantomime* is used in the world of animation is probably a holdover from the days of the silent cartoons. Back then, the characters *did* use pantomime! But that's because they had no voices, no other way to communicate. All that changed when talkies came in. Today, it is common for the animator—particularly in feature animation—to listen to a prerecorded voice track, making his animation fit the voices. And when you do that, you're really not pantomiming. You're looking for the motivation underneath the words. Remember that words express thoughts. If the animator is trying to pantomime the words he is hearing, he is going to wind up trying to physically convey the words in a wordless way. Words, movement, and emotion do not fit together like that, even in animation.

Speaking actors don't pantomime and, in fact, it is considered to be bad acting if they do. It is too external, too much of an "indication" of emotion rather than a straightforward expression of it. The movement in pantomime is very—for lack of a better word—artful, and the audience relates to it differently than they do to the general movement of speaking actors. There is an added mental step in pantomime. Part of the appreciation is in the "considered" nature of the movement.

Charlie Chaplin considered himself to be a pantomime, which he defined as a performer who would use gestures and facial expressions to convey emotion. That's because he worked in silent pictures but, frankly, I think he underestimated himself. He was far more than a mime. Chaplin was always a powerful actor, attuned to generating a sense of empathy in his international audience. Taking his self-assessment at face value, however, may explain why his stardom diminished with the advent of sound in motion pictures. To be sure, sound is what killed certain animated, pantomimed characters, like Felix the Cat. And other silent stars like Harry Langdon and Buster Keaton did not make the transition because they mainly practiced pantomime. In Chaplin's autobiography, he bemoans the arrival of sound pictures, and he delayed his participation in it for as long as he could.

As we have already discussed, acting has very little to do with words anyway. It's all about intention, motivation, actions—emotion. But if character movement takes the form of pantomime, you've crossed over into another distinct art form.

Laban Movement Theory

Rudolf Laban (1879–1958) was a major pioneer in the Central European Expressionist Art modern dance movement. He developed a new and influential approach to the study of dance, focusing on the systematic analysis of movement in relation to the dynamic use of the body in space. He also created a widely used form of notation (now evolved into Labanotation) to describe movement. Laban's work was revolutionary in its day and has subsequently been applied to a wide variety of disciplines, from psychotherapy to ethnology, from movement therapy to voice training, acting, and dance and, during the past several years, to computer animation. Although there is no school or teacher offering specific Laban movement training for animators at this time, animator and Certified Laban Movement Analyst Leslie Bishko, Director of the Computer Animation Program at Vancouver Institute of Media Arts in Canada, has written several papers on the application of Laban Movement Analysis (LMA) to computer animation methods. She includes analogies between Laban's Effort theory and the twelve Animation Principles. I am indebted to Ms. Bishko and to Jean Newlove of the Jean Newlove Centre for Laban Studies in London for their assistance in preparing the following primer.

Before getting into Laban theory itself, a brief historical preface is helpful because Rudolf Laban's original ideas have been interpreted, reinterpreted, and synthesized in different ways in different parts of the world at different times by different folks. Jean Newlove studied personally with Rudolf Laban in the 1940s, worked as his assistant and is familiar with what the man himself had to say. She is the author of an excellent book on the subject, entitled *Laban for Actors and Dancers* (1993). Her school offers a diploma course in which students study Laban in depth, using it as a base for most theatre skills. Simultaneous with Newlove's career in Britain and Europe, however, Laban's theories found their way to the United States through other disciples. Imgard Bartenieff in particular mixed her perspectives with Laban's and created Laban Movement Analysis (LMA), a theoretical framework for movement observation and description for which

Laban movement theory

one can receive certification through the Laban/Bartenieff Institute of Movement Studies in New York. Graduates from this school have fanned out across the United States and Canada and have, in turn, trained others. Animator Leslie Bishko studied the LMA branch of Laban, not Laban theory as espoused by Ms. Newlove. While there are differences in terminology and focus between the North American and British versions of Laban theory, their roots are very similar.

That's enough history. Let's roll up our sleeves and get to work. I can't possibly do justice to this very rich resource in these few pages, but I want to give you the basic ideas behind Laban theory, plus a list of resources for further study.

It is difficult to talk about movement because it is constantly changing. Imagine the challenge you would face if you had to write a paper describing in detail how a child's body is moving as he pedals his tricycle up and down the driveway. He's pedaling like crazy, then he slows down, and then he topples over as he tries to make a U-turn. At every point, the nature of his movement changes. The genius of Rudolf Laban is that he defined a set of movement categories, with parameters within each category. These parameters provide a frame of reference for the observation and description of movement. In this chapter, I introduce two categories: *space* (i.e., where the movement is happening) and *effort* (i.e., how intention and will affect movement).

The CD-ROM that accompanies this book contains a picture of a twenty-sided object called an *icosahedron*. Along with the tetrahedron and three others, the icosahedron is one of Plato's solids, and it is at the base of Rudolf Laban's theories.

Space

Imagine that you have created an animated character that looks like a regular-sized brick with arms and legs, and it is standing in the icosahedron. In Laban terminology, the personal space around your character is called its *kinesphere*—the distance it can extend its arms and its free leg if it is balancing on one leg. Your character can move to any of the twenty points of the icosahedron. Actually, your character can move in infinite ways but, for the purposes of this chapter—and for simplicity's sake—I will reduce this to the most basic six movements: (1) forward, (2) backward, (3) up, (4) down, (5) sideways/left, (6) sideways/right. Forward/backward movement occurs on the sagittal axis; up/down movement occurs on the vertical axis; left/right movement occurs on the horizontal axis.

As Leslie Bishko observes, "the axes are directly analogous to the Cartesian coordinate system's X, Y, and Z axes, used in computer animation."

Effort

Effort refers to *how* the character moves through space. She can move in different ways, depending on how you vary her inner attitude toward space, time, and weight. Each character you create is unique and moves in his or her own way, right? She can move on a Time scale measured from very fast urgency to very lingering slowness; she mobilizes her Weight with forceful strength or delicate lightness, and her attention toward Space can be direct, like an arrow, or indirect, like a mangled figure eight. Plus there is the variable of Flow, a factor that pertains to the "feeling" of movement and can be measured on a scale that ranges from Bound to Free. When a baseball pitcher winds up for a pitch, for example, his movement has a Bound quality. It has resistance, a pause, and then the ball is hurled across home plate with Free Flow, as if he is trying to throw the ball straight through the catcher's mitt.

Let's look a little closer at the Time factor, break it down a little further. This offers a way to differentiate between *qualitative* time (sudden, urgent or sustained, lingering) and *quantitative* time (fast, slow, accelerating, decelerating). If the brick character you created walks down a city street, her movement may be sudden (urgent) or sustained (lingering), accelerating or decelerating, depending on circumstance. If she steps around a pothole, she may slow down; or she may speed up to make the traffic light. This being the case, both Leslie Bishko and Jean Newlove prefer to refer to the Time continuum as one ranging from suddenness to sustainment, with the presumption that the character may, while moving suddenly or sustained, vary between fast and slow.

It is useful to think of Effort as the character's "inner attitude" toward the movement factors of Space, Weight, Time, and Flow. It's not the mass of the thing or character that makes the difference, but the character's attitude toward how it moves. For example, when considering Weight, the character can have an Active or Passive attitude toward mobilization of his body weight. Imgard Bartenieff (LMA) is the one who originally came up with the distinctions between Active and Passive. As she put it, "Lightness in Passive Weight becomes Limp; Strong Passive Weight becomes Heaviness, giving in." The British version of Laban does not use these terms, preferring Rudolf's original *resisting* or *indulging*. But regardless of the precise terminology, you get the idea. The character can be active or passive, give in to or resist movement.

Does your character move with quick, flicking motions or with slow purposeful movement? There are eight possible combinations of Space, Time, Weight, and Flow, all of which are demonstrated by an actor who appears in the CD-ROM that accompanies this book. If we remove Flow from the equation, which has to do with the emotional or "feeling" aspects of movement, we wind up with the following basic types of movement:

Press	(direct, sustained, strong)
Wring	(indirect, sustained, strong)
Glide	(direct, sustained, light)
Float	(indirect, sustained, light)
Thrust	(direct, sudden, strong)
Slash	(indirect, sudden, strong)
Dab	(direct, sudden, light)
Flick	(indirect, sudden, light)

The best and easiest way to really grasp how this works is to get up on your feet and move around the room. Reading about Laban is like reading about bicycle riding. It's all well and good to know how the chain goes 'round and 'round but, at some point, you need to get up on the bike to really grasp what it means to ride the thing. I know it looks silly to dance around the room, but forget about that. You're an artist, and artists are already thought to be a bit odd.

First, just relax and walk with ease from one side of the room to the other, like your regular self. Don't try to be a character or to otherwise change yourself. Be aware of your body as you move through the space.

Now let's transfer your weight and keep walking. When we talk about varying the "weight" of a character, we're referring to a tension that exists between gravity and upward movement. Relaxation equates to weight. Totally relax, and you'll fall down on the ground. A drunken person is relaxed, pulled down by gravity. When you are having an energetic day, your energy will lift you up, pushing away from gravity. Exuberance pushes you away from gravity.

Let's work on Pressing. Think of it like pushing a friend's stalled car off to the side of the road. Direct, sustained, strong. See? Do it. You'd push a car differently than you would a shopping cart, which would be closer to Gliding.

Now try Wringing. Suppose you are yourself a soaking towel. If you wring yourself out, you do so in an indirect, sustained, and strong manner.

Floating is what it sounds like it is. Balloons float. Remember boxer Mohammed Ali in his prime? "I float like a butterfly, sting like a bee!" he used to shout in the ring. In Laban terms, Mohammed would be Floating (indirect + sustained + light), and then Thrusting (direct + sudden+ strong), maybe interspersed with Flicking (indirect + sudden + light).

If you were a cotton ball being dabbed onto somebody's face, how would you move? What is Dabbing? Direct, sudden, and light. Got it?

From the animator's perspective, movement is the visible outer result of the character's inner impulses. If you animate that brick you created earlier, causing him to walk in a jaunty, brisk, and determined fashion, light on his feet, chest out, the person viewing the animation would presume this is a happy character. This movement could be described as Dabbing. Are you starting to see how Laban can be used?

Phrasing, which is a term much used by Leslie Bishko, refers to the rhythmic changes of movement in an animated character. Changes of Effort over time can be phrased in the following ways:

Even:	continuous, unchanging
Increasing:	from lesser to greater intensity, accelerating
Decreasing:	from greater to lesser intensity, decelerating
Accented:	series of accents
Vibratory:	series of sudden, repetitive movements
Resilient:	series of rebounding, resilient movements (Maletic 1984)

Applying this quality to the animated brick walking down the street, we could say his phrasing is "even," perhaps "increasing," if you want to show a growing sense of urgency.

In my conversation with Leslie Bishko when preparing this chapter, she said, "My teaching is infused with LMA-esque scrutiny of animated movement. The LMA themes that come up over and over again are Initiation/Sequencing and Phrasing. In particular, the phrase Anticipation-Squash/Stretch-Follow-Through-Overlapping is a practical example of LMA's phrasing principle of Preparation/Action/Recuperation. I also discuss the elasticity of Squash and Stretch in relationship to Breath and Shape changes in the torso to help students understand how they can phrase their use of Squash and Stretch to convey emotion" (1999).

Laban theory is a big, important, and largely unexplored subject for both animators and actors. It is my fervent hope that the publication of this book will spur more research and further application. Jean Newlove's orientation is with motivation for actors and dancers, artists who get up on their feet and actually move through space. The actor in me responds powerfully to this perspective. Leslie Bishko's LMA orientation is with computer animators, artists who manipulate characters on a screen. Her goal is to create an industry-standard computer animation interface based on LMA—for animators to better describe and analyze movement. They are both, however, concerned with how the mind/body expresses processes that manifest themselves in movement, and, with both acting and animation, that is Ground Zero.

Speech
6

Acting has very little to do with words. Words express a thought, the same as a hug or a kiss. What we are really searching for in acting is intention, objectives, motivation, and emotion. In other words, acting is more about what is *underneath* the words. Remember the metaphor of the iceberg: Only 15 percent of it shows above the water line; 85 percent is under the water. But in order for it to be an iceberg, you still have to have the unseen 85 percent.

Animators who work in feature films have a tough job because the character voices are typically recorded before the animation is created. In the real world, movement precedes words. When a thought occurs, it is not the words that emerge first, it is head and eye movement, shoulder and neck movement. Therefore, when animating to prerecorded dialogue, the animator is forced to sort of work backward from the way actors work, finding the inner impulse—the thought—that would be expressed by the recorded words. In the instant before a character speaks, he moves, expressing the impulse. Watch the way ventriloquists make their dummies move around, looking this way and that, generally a beat ahead of the mouth movement.

Here's a trick I use all the time in my regular acting classes, one that may help you find the key to animating a prerecorded voice. Listen for the most awkward or most difficult or most unusual word or phrase in a scene. Isolate it and say it out loud yourself. Try to find in yourself the impulse that would allow you to express this way. If you can justify that, you can probably hang the rest of the character on it. Let's say you're listening to a voice track in which a male character says at one point, "Oh, goody, goody, goody!!" Now, you probably don't walk around in your daily life saying that. It wouldn't be cool. But try it on for size. Get up from your chair and walk around the room, saying out loud, "Oh, goody, goody, goody!!" You'll discover that the impulse comes from a high place in the body, for starters, and you'll probably want to purse your lips when you say it. The character is a lip purser who carries his energy up in the shoulder and neck area. Also, keep in mind when you are animating a prerecorded dialogue track that movement and emotion are a two-way street. Emotion makes you move a certain way, and the way you move will make you feel a certain way.

Since the audience expects to hear dialogue once the impulse to speak is evident, there is comedy to be found in putting a delay between the impulse and the actual audible sound. Find the impulse to speak, but then don't speak. Hold the impulse, ride it like a pony. The audience will hang on the moment with great expectancy. If you have a prerecorded track, it's difficult to use this one because the timing is already built in, but maybe one day you'll get the chance. I recall years ago seeing a production of William Sayoran's *The Time of Your Life*. One of the characters had a philosophical and rather nonsensical short speech to give: "What? What not? No foundation, all the way down the line." The actor playing the role stretched that one sequence into maybe a minute and a half of hysterically funny, shifting inner impulses. He would find the impulse to say something, then decide not to say that, changing the impulse to another thought and predictor-movement, then deciding not to say that. And of course, by the time he finally finished, what he said hadn't made much sense anyway. It was fall-down-on-the-floor funny. Try it yourself. You can hold an audience on the tip of your fingers for a very long time this way. If they feel you are about to say something, they'll hang in there with you. I've never seen an animator use the lesson, but there is no reason why it would not work there, too.

The Look of Memory

We remember things in specifics, not generalities. If I asked you to remember a special summer vacation from your childhood, you would retrieve from your memory a bunch of mental snapshots and images—one special moment from the vacation, then another. Maybe the snapshots would include the moment when you and your girlfriend were down by the dock, sharing lunch, tossing pebbles in the water. The sun was pushing through an overcast sky. The air was humid. The trees and shrubs across the way were a deeper green than usual, still damp from the earlier thunderstorm. Snapshots: her smile, the kiss, your feet dangling in the water—a moment in time. And then you say to me, "Yeah, that was a great summer." It is impossible to remember the entire summer all at one time. Thoughts occur one after another, not all at the same time.

Understanding the way memory works is important to animators because there is a particular kind of expression on the face of a person who is remembering something. A bad actor "indicates" the act of remembering. He'll scratch his head, stroke his chin whiskers and say, "Why, sure . . . I remember that summer." But when a person *really* remembers something, he doesn't do all that indicating. On the contrary, the act of remembering—especially something that is in the deep past—tends to *still* a person, not animate him.

Not only does a face involved in remembering become more still, but also the eyes shift in predictable ways. Let's say you have to animate a character that is remembering something from long ago, like maybe his childhood in the farmyard or school days in Minsk. When we recall a memory, we actually "see" it all over again, and it causes our eyeballs to do funny things. Try this experiment: Describe to me what you did when you got out of bed this morning. In your mind's eye, you will suddenly be transported to the perspective of a fly on the wall of your bedroom. You'll "see" yourself lying in bed, waking up, shifting your feet to the floor. Remember doing that? Good. Notice how, as you "saw" this memory, your eyes actually shifted off to the side and slightly upward? Well, they did. Try it on a friend. Recent memory causes the eyes to shift upward and to the side. More distant memory, like what the dashboard looked like on the first car you owned, will cause the eyes to shift downward and to the side. It's almost as if the more distant the memory, the deeper into yourself you have to look to find it.

When you remember something, you do not continue to gaze straight ahead. I can tell you're skeptical about this, so don't take my word for it. Try it with a friend. Ask her to tell you about her bas mitzvah or something, get her to describe the room the party was in. Watch her eyes shift as she remembers.

When I'm teaching acting, I can always tell if a student is faking a memory sequence by the focus of his eyes. If he continues to stare straight out at the audience while he is remembering, then I know he is only *acting* like he is remembering. He's not doing the real McCoy.

Making certain that a character's eyes shift in the correct direction in the context of the memory is important. If you get it wrong, the audience will not catch the mistake.

But they will know something is just not quite right. The moment doesn't ring true. Send the eyes in the wrong direction, and you'll be losing empathy.

Active Listening

Imagine a scene set in Washington Square Park in New York, on a sunny summer morning. The characters are two middle-aged women who are sitting next to one another on a bench, talking about their kids who are playing in the fountain. They take turns talking, sometimes interrupting one another. The trick to making this kind of transaction come alive is *active listening*. When Woman #1 talks, Woman #2 does more than just sit there, absorbing. Woman #2 is listening, projecting ahead, filling in blanks that are left unsaid, framing responses, deciding not to interrupt, and keeping an eye on her kid. In other words, listening, when it is right, is extremely active.

Actor Nicol Williamson tells a story about when he was a young actor, playing his first large role. In the play, his character first entered a party scene at the top of the play, but he didn't speak any lines for two pages. After a run-through, the director was giving notes to the assembled cast. "Nicol, what are you doing during your first entrance, after you enter the party?" "You mean before I speak? I'm not doing anything really, just listening." "Wrong," said the director. "You're listening, coming up with responses to what is being said—and then deciding not to say them." The point is that, even for those two pages of nonspeaking, it was essential for the actor to be *doing* something. If a tornado had blown through the Evil Queen's palace while she was stirring her bubbling, festering pot of poison, she would have had to stop doing what she was doing and deal with the storm, close windows and such. She would then be playing another action, this one not in pursuit of being the fairest one of all, but of staying alive. Once secure, she would return to her poisons and her evil objectives.

When one character listens to another, he should still be "doing" something. In fact, your character should be doing something 100 percent of the time when he is on stage. *Doing* means playing an action, pursuing an objective. Scratching an ear or crossing a leg is also doing something, but that's not what I mean. To *do* something, theatrically speaking, is to play an action, to have intention, to pursue an objective.

The Camera

7

Acting for the Camera

In live-action movies, the reaction shot is important. It is so important, in fact, that many live-action actors view the master shot as little more than a rehearsal for the close-ups. When editing a movie, the editor usually cuts to reaction shots. In close-up coverage of a shot, in fact, they learn to "listen, react, speak"—being careful not to overlap lines. This is so the editors can get a clean edit on the sound track and will have reaction shots to cut to.

The basic setup for a filmed live-action scene is a "master shot," which includes the action of the entire scene, plus "coverage"—close-ups this way and close-ups that way. It is all put together in the editing room. An animated movie, of course, doesn't shoot the same way. It's not necessary to make an animated master shot for an entire scene, plus entire-scene close-ups. You lay all that out on the story board in the first place, essentially editing beforehand. But, to the extent that an animated feature film follows live-action film-editing technique, it is useful to talk for a minute about the way actors in live action approach the process. The performance they give in a master shot is different from what they do in a close-up.

A master shot is usually photographed from some distance, anywhere from a few feet to the length of a football field. The further away the shot is, the more physical the actor can—and must—be. It is okay to gesture a lot, for example, if the master shot is staged across the distance of a department store parking lot. At that distance, the actor would think of it as delivering a performance that is almost as large as what he might do on the Broadway stage.

The closer the camera gets to the actor, the more still the performance needs to be. In extreme close-up, when you have a full screen of the actor's face, everything is in the eyes, so you don't want to have the character's head shaking around too much.

Acting for the camera

The camera sees thoughts. The audience and other characters will likely look first at the eyes for clues about emotional state. One caveat: In your effort to make the character hold still, be careful that you don't lower the emotional stakes! This is a very common error made by new actors when they first start acting for camera. The intention is the same as in the long shot, the stakes remain high, but the *focus* of the performance is different.

The point is this: when you are animating a sequence that includes long shots and close-ups, remember that the actor behaves differently depending on the shot. You don't simply take the action from the long shot and blow it up because, if you do, the physical action would be too frenetic in close-up. Make the performance the right size for the frame of the shot.

Elia Kazan, the director of such classic movies as *A Streetcar Named Desire, On the Waterfront,* and *East of Eden,* says that the camera doesn't just look at the actor, it looks inside him (1988, 256). What he means by this is that the camera sees the tapestry of thoughts and emotions inside the character. One of my favorite contemporary movie actors is Kevin Spacey (*Swimming with Sharks, American Beauty*). The thing that makes him so good on camera is the way he performs in close-up. When the camera cuts to him for a reaction, it typically sees the reaction, and then his reaction evolves into yet another thought. It's mental and emotional movement, caught on film. This mental fluidity makes him appear more interesting than the line of the script might suggest.

The Actor Generally Leads the Camera

The camera's perspective in a master shot is usually that of an audience. Camera movement is led by the actor's gaze or shift of attention. For example, consider the following scene: In the master shot, a woman sits at a table in a restaurant, alone, waiting for someone. She glances at her watch. Move in for medium-close shot so we pick up her facial expression. Whoever she is waiting for is late. Off-camera, we hear a female voice: "Sorry I'm late. . . ." The woman at the table reacts to the voice and looks toward the door. Cut to: Woman's POV of friend approaching table. Or, the camera might pan toward the door, following the woman's glance, picking up her friend as she enters the scene.

Now suppose the scene had been shot this way: Same master shot. Same medium-close up. But instead of hearing the friend's greeting off-camera while the on-screen shot captures the seated woman's reaction, we quick-cut to the woman at the door, entering. She sees her friend at the table and, from her recognition, she calls out, "Sorry I'm late. . . ." Then we cut to the woman at the table, reacting to the arrival of her friend.

We could do it either way and the scene would work, but we'd have to put in the reaction shots somewhere.

Imagine a scene in a haunted house, late afternoon. Our hero climbs the creaking wooden steps, pushes thick cobwebs aside, and steps into the main entrance hall. Silence and gloom. Slow pan around the room from our hero's POV, sunlight casting oddly shaped shadows through the dust. Cut back to hero, taking in the room, smelling the mustiness. Suddenly, a large bat comes to life in the rafters, his flapping wings in turn disturbing some nesting birds that fly into action, squawking. Cut to our alarmed hero, reacting to the noise, looking around anxiously. Cut back to the room. Birds fly out a broken window, the bat settles back into the rafters. Cut back to hero. His face, now touched with a glaze of perspiration, relaxes. He chuckles at his own skittishness and continues cautiously into the house.

Sergei Eisenstein (1898–1948), the great Russian director, outlined the challenge faced by film directors. "Our films are faced with the task of presenting not only a narrative that is logically connected," he said, "but one that contains a maximum of emotion and stimulating power" (Eisenstein 1942, 4). He then answered the challenge: "The basic fact . . . remains true to this day, that the juxtaposition of two separate shots by slicing them together resembles not so much a simple sum of one shot plus another shot as it does a creation" (7).

Film is, in my opinion, a far more manipulative medium than is the stage. The director takes a more aggressive posture, telling the audience to "Look here, at this surprised face!" or "Look over there at that being being bathed." Or "Stand way back and take in the whole panorama, and now, quickly, look very closely at the young woman carrying laundry out of the wood shack." Since Walt Disney, animation and live action have been joined at the hip. If you want to understand the power of the former, study the latter. In my Acting for Animators workshops, frequently it's the screening of live-action film clips that make the greatest impact on the animators.

Technique 8

Technique is a potpourri category of acting dos and don'ts. An actor learns, for example, that if a scene is going south, if he's starting to hear people in the audience coughing and shuffling around, the worst thing to do is to "chase" them, to increase the intensity of the performance. That will only make it worse. It is preferable to stop, reconnect with your intention and scene partner—and the audience will return. In short: "Don't chase your audience!" Animators, of course, don't have this sort of problem to solve because animation isn't presented to an audience in real-time, but there are many snippets of acting wisdom that I think you will be able to use in animation.

If you read entertainment industry trade publications, you'll see advertisements for acting teachers who teach Meisner Technique or Adler Technique or even Stanislavsky Technique. Lee Strasberg's Method acting could be called a technique. None of this means much except that each teacher advocates his own approach to acting and has slapped his name on it in order to sell more seats in their classes. There is in reality no single, correct "Technique." Technique is whatever works.

Simplify Your Actions

The more direct, simple, and specific your acting choices are, the better. Trying to play, for example, "I want to be loved," is neither active nor specific enough. A stronger choice would be "I want you to go on a date with me" or "I want you to marry me." It might be true that your character "needs" love and affection, which gives voltage to the way he tries to get a date, but it is a weak acting choice to play the general need instead of the specific action.

Avoid Ambivalence

When you have to animate a character that is having an indecisive moment, it is stronger to have him shift between two strong convictions than it is for him to be ambivalent. In other words, if your character is uncertain whether to kiss the girl or not, it is best to have him commit 100 percent to "I'm going to do it!!"—and then have him shift 100 percent the other direction with "What am I doing? Am I crazy?!!" The alternative is to have him just sit there, his internal dialogue being, "Oh me, oh my! I don't know what to do. . . ." Shifting back and forth between strong decisions, even if it is done with lightning-quick speed, is more dynamic acting-wise. Imagine a character that comes to a fork in the road. Which way to go? Left or right? Mentally, switch back and forth until a decision is made.

Never Deny the Reality of Your Scene Partner

What this means is that, even if you are absolutely certain how your character should be acting, be prepared to change depending on what your scene partner is doing. My understanding is that some animators are assigned individual characters, and others are assigned scenes with multiple characters. If you are doing the latter, then this note won't mean much to you because you are controlling the behavior of all the characters. But if you are responsible for only one character, he won't exist in a vacuum, and his behavior will vary depending on his scene partner.

What Kind of Animal Would Your Character Be?

I could have put this under "Movement," but it's not something you use every single time you act. For me, it falls better under "Technique," something to rely on when you can't get a handle on a character. The premise is actually simple: Think of your human character as an animal. What kind of animal would he be? When I saw Tommy Lee Jones play the law in the movie *The Fugitive*, I noticed he continually sniffed the air, just like a wolf. Alma in Tennessee Williams' play *Summer and Smoke* is birdlike, maybe a stork or a heron—skittish, wary, but regal. Dustin Hoffman had an early triumph in a movie entitled *Midnight Cowboy*. Rent it some time, it's a good flick. Observe how Hoffman's character, Ratso Rizzo, actually moves like a rat. That's not an accident.

For the animator, this saw can cut both ways. If you're animating an animal, ask yourself what kind of *human* he would be.

Remember the Fruit Salad

After watching an actress perform in a scene at the Actor's Studio, Lee Strasberg determined that she was making an acting error. As she stood on stage, awaiting his sage advice, he asked her an odd question. "Do you know how to make a fruit salad?" She figured she hadn't heard him correctly. "Excuse me?" "A fruit salad," he repeated, "Do you know how to make one?" "Well, yes." "How do you do it?" The actress was nonplussed, aware that the entire packed room was watching her. She could not fathom how this line of questioning had anything at all to do with her acting. "Umm . . . well, I peel a banana . . ." She paused. "Yes? Then what?" "Well, I cut up some strawberries and a few grapes, maybe put in some grapefruit, perhaps a peach. . . ." "And then you have a fruit salad, right?" asked Strasberg, peering at the girl through his thick glasses. "Uh-huh." "Good," Strasberg beamed. "That's the mistake you were making with that scene. You were trying to have a fruit salad before you had done all the things with the fruit."

When you are animating a character, it is absolutely essential that he or she go through all of the thoughts that the scene calls for. No shortcuts. You can have the thoughts come through like lightning, but they must all be there. This is a very important acting lesson. Remember Strasberg's fruit salad, and do not play the end of the scene before you get there. Suppose you're working on a character for a Jell-O commercial, and he has to take a bite and say, "Yum!" The thought process goes this way: As the spoon comes toward the mouth, the character is looking forward to the bite based on his preconceived idea of what Jell-O tastes like. There is expectation. Once he takes the Jell-O into his mouth, there is a moment of tasting, after which the communication goes to the brain. Jell-O is good! From the brain, the word *Yum!* comes out the mouth. You see what I mean? It's not a simple matter of "spoon in—big grin—spoon out—*Yum!*" There is a sequence of thoughts and reactions that come with the taste.

Live-Action Reference

Feature animation usually involves animating the characters after the voice track is recorded. And most voice-over sessions are videotaped for later reference. The animator can watch the tape and observe the body language and facial expressions of the actor when he actually recorded the words. This is a valuable live-action reference, but it has some limitations that are worth mentioning.

Speaking now as an actor who has done my share of voice-over work, I'm here to tell you that what an actor does with a line in front of a microphone in a recording studio is not necessarily what he would do with that same line if he was playing a scene on location or on stage. A lot of the variable comes from the recording-session necessity that the actor remain close to the microphone and not to make extraneous noises. The engineers want a clean track. What this means is that actors who are doing voice recordings will focus all of their bodily energy in support of the words being recorded—instead of playing off the reality of an actual scene partner. I, for example, will use my arms and hands far more in a recording session than I might in the actual playing of a scene with another actor. And my face will tend to be more animated because I'm trying to summon up 100 percent of the emotion that might be expressed by the words I'm recording. An actor in a recording session is, in a way, playing to himself, and the animator is wise to take this into consideration when watching videotapes of his performance.

Rotoscoping

Rotoscoping—making a direct copy or tracing of a filmed or taped live-action performance—is, by definition, a second-generation performance, so you're already swimming upstream if you want to create a sense of theatrical spontaneity in the animation. And, if that isn't troubling enough, there is the real possibility that the original live-action performance you are rotoscoping lacked a "feeling for acting" in the first place.

Directing real, live actors is an art in itself, hard enough to do when the final goal is to put the live-action performances up on the screen. But to direct live action with the goal being to have it later copied into animation . . . yikes! That's tough. If the director of a live-action sequence is oriented to the final animation—in other words, if he is focusing on the ultimate performance of the animators instead of focusing on the in-the-present-moment performance of the live actors—he may be tempted to push for lots of physical movement, even if it is not motivated acting-wise.

There is a real trap waiting in the capture of live-action movement for movement's sake, especially if it is segregated from theatrical intention and the actor-audience contract. It is sort of like studying the movement of a person riding a bicycle without taking into consideration where he is going on the bike. Legs move up and down, body hunkers over the handlebars, breath goes in and out of lungs. . . . But a person who is riding to town to fetch the doctor is going to ride that bike a whole lot differently from someone who is riding a stationary bike at a health club. Intention affects emotion, emotion affects movement.

Disney animators Frank Thomas and Ollie Johnston, in their book, *The Illusion of Life*, talk despairingly about their efforts with rotoscoping. "Whenever we stayed too close to the Photostats, or directly copied even a tiny piece of human action, the results looked very strange. The moves appeared real enough, but the figure lost the illusion of life. . . . The point is," they continue, "a work of art is never a copy; for it to have meaning to people of many generations and numerous cultures, it must be the personal statement of the artist" (Thomas and Johnston 1981, 252–53). Indeed. The illusion of life is in the character's emotion and the artist's interpretation of reality—not in the isolated movement of various body parts.

Mocap, Schomocap

Motion Capture, otherwise known in the trade as *mocap*, is a CG descendant of rotoscope, which was invented by Max Fleischer for 2-D purposes. It involves the wiring up of a live actor, dancer, or mime with sensors so that his movements are converted into a digitized computer map. He raises his left arm and, on the screen, the image raises its left arm. He shakes his head, and the image shakes its head.

Once the performance is thus "captured," it falls to the animator to take the computer image and enhance it to make it into animation. The basic movement is already taken care of, so the animators just has to fill in the blanks, so to speak. The public is supposed to be none the wiser, and the entire enterprise is said to be a big money-saver for the producers.

Most animators actively hate mocap because it puts them into a secondary position creatively. The live performers have already delivered the essence—and what is worse, the live performance itself may well be lacking if its focus is on movement rather than performance. In some of the live action that was rotoscoped for Disney's feature film *Pocahontas*, for example, the actress was actually a dancer. When she walked across the room in some the live-action reference scenes, she did so like a dancer—toes out, ball-of-foot down first—not like a regular person.

Motion Capture is used widely in computer games and, in feature films, for background crowd scenes (*Titanic* is a good example) and stunts (*Batman*). It is controversial because so many grandiose, even incorrect claims have been made about its virtues as a cost-saving replacement for the character animator. The truth is that mocap can be very expensive and is not at all a replacement for the character animator. Also, it comes with a number of limitations, mainly that you can only use it for human figures. You can't capture a human and then turn that into animation for an animal. Further, you can't capture the motion of a skinny person and turn it into animation for a fat person because weight moves differently with skinny and fat.

For an excellent overview and history of Motion Capture, I strongly recommend *Understanding Motion Capture for Computer Animation and Video Games* by Alberto Menache (2000). Alberto, currently the Character Technical Direction Supervisor at Pacific Data Images, has been working with Motion Capture for many years, and his book is the most eloquent and final word on the subject.

There isn't much I can do except commiserate with animators who have to clean up and enhance a mocap performance, but I'd like to share a few thoughts with the folks who direct the live-action performances in the first place.

Actors perform for audiences. The thing that actors do *presumes* an audience. Acting is an interpretative art, from actor to audience. So when you are directing performers for mocap (or video reference), follow this blueprint, even if you are working on a kick boxing computer game:

1. What does the character want? What does he/she need?

2. What is the character's relationship with the other performers?

3. What is the "moment before"? In other words, where did the character come from when he entered the scene?

4. What is the "moment after"? In other words, where is the character going after he leaves the scene?

5. Where is the audience in relation to the performer? Actors play for an audience, one way or the other, even if they are acting in movies. Even though you may want to capture a lot of motion on the computer, it will help to tell the performer where the audience is.

6. A scene is a negotiation. Where is the negotiation in the scene?

Character Rhythm

You can actually tap out a person's or character's inner rhythm with a pencil on the desk. A sloth or snail would have, naturally, a much slower inner rhythm than a woodpecker. The rhythm of a character can change based on circumstances. What happens, do you figure, when a sloth gets angry? Same inner rhythm? I don't think so. The sloth won't suddenly start jumping around like a rabbit, and he probably will still move about a foot a day—but you should be able to tell by looking at him that his inner rhythm has increased. It would be in the eyes, maybe the set of the jaw.

Mirrors

Want to create a firestorm in a room full of animators? Walk in there and suggest that they get rid of their mirrors. Animators love mirrors! They like to make facial expressions in them, act out scenes in front of them. Little mirrors, big mirrors, hand mirrors, full-length mirrors—animators will usually have one close at hand. Actors, by contrast, quickly learn to *avoid* mirrors. It's a left-brain/right-brain problem. As soon as you shift your brain into a watching mode, you stop acting. The moment you wanted to watch is gone, and a new moment has arrived. You wind up standing there with a silly expression on your face, in a freeze frame. What's going on? Are mirrors good or bad for acting? Useful or not? Rather than providing a hard-and-fast rule, running the risk of turning up the heat even further, let me simply offer a perspective that high-lights one of the fundamental differences between the way that live actors and anima-tors approach acting.

It is literally and physically impossible to be 100 percent actor and 100 percent audience simultaneously. The problem with acting into a mirror is that you are trying to force an impossible situation, splitting off part of your brain to watch what the reflection of what rest of you is doing. Since live actors aspire to be 100 percent "in the moment" when they act, rehearsing in front of a mirror is a path that leads in the wrong direction—to duality. Philosopher Denis Diderot (1713–1784) wrote a famous treatise entitled *The Paradox of Acting*, in which he asserted that all acting actually has dual-ity, that no matter how much an actor tries, he can never be 100 percent in the moment (Diderot 2000, 198–201). If he succeeded, blocking out all other conscious considerations, he might just wander off the stage or maybe hurt somebody in the big murder scene. Diderot correctly pointed out that an actor must always have a control-ling distance from his performance. Indeed, an audience requires that the actor be in control of his performance. If the actor appears out of control on stage, it makes the audience nervous.

Diderot's theory of duality is the wiggle-room in which animators do their mirror thing. Animators do not have a live audience to give them immediate feedback, and so they act for the audience in their heads. Duality—doing and watching at the same time—works a lot better for animators than it does for actors.

Mirrors are a good way for the animator to check and analyze poses, broad action, facial expression, that kind of thing—but you'll get into trouble if you try to actually act "in the present moment" while watching yourself in the mirror. In other words, if you try to go through an entire full-body scene. For one thing, you will necessarily have your face turned toward the mirror so you can watch yourself, which may not be appropriate for the scene.

Live actors are taught not to think about externals or "results." Facial expressions are "results." If I hit your toe with a hammer, you'll make a facial expression without thinking about it. If you sniff a vial of ammonia or a skunk in the woods, you'll make a face without thinking about it. An animator has a different kind of problem: He will say to himself, "My character smells a skunk. Now what kind of face would he make?"—at which point he gets out the mirror out of the desk drawer and wrinkles up his nose for inspection. An actor would consider this to be "indicating," or playing a "result." An actor would not say to himself, "I need to let the audience know I smell something bad. . . . hmmmmm . . . What kind of expression can I make?" Instead, he would actually smell something, the air in the room probably, and play mental tricks on himself to pretend the smell is obnoxious.

The issue with mirrors, from an actor's perspective, is that if he watches himself in a mirror, he'll be tempted to re-create that look or expression on stage or in front of the movie camera. And that would not be acting at all, but a form of mimicry. ("Lessee . . . the bad odor facial expression goes like this. . . .")

The proof for animators is in the pudding of course. Mirrors have been a valuable hand tool for many years, and if they work for you, then keep using them. If you really want to see how facial expressions and body movement occurs naturally, it would be better to videotape yourself acting out a scene, and then to replay the tape for study. But that would generally be too time-consuming. So go ahead and use the mirror. But keep in mind the limitations.

The Form
9

Comedy

The animator should know what creates laughter—why do things appeal to people as being funny.

—Walt Disney memo to Don Graham, December 23, 1935

If what you're doing is funny, you don't have to be funny doing it.

—Charlie Chaplin

There is only one way of making comedy richer—and, paradoxically, funnier—and that is by making it more serious.

—Walter Kerr, *The Silent Clowns*

I confess that, as an actor, comedy is my Achilles' heel. I can be a funny guy on stage and, at times, I enjoy my own performance too much. Once I get an audience laughing, the temptation is to say to them, in effect, "Hell, if you think that was funny, take a look at this!"—at which point I try to top myself and, of course, the laughter dries right up. The audience doesn't like it if the actor laughs at himself or points too overtly to the joke. They want to participate, to use their imagination, and if the actor is telling them where the laughs are, they get insulted.

If you want to find the comedy in a scene, forget about being funny and ask yourself what is true. What is the scene really about? What do the characters want? Where is the negotiation? If you're trying to be funny, you're on the same slippery slope that carried the Keystone Kops into oblivion.

Lift the hood of any good comedy, and you'll find the engine of a good drama. This is why, when a person decides to become an actor, his training usually begins with drama, not comedy. Comedy is harder than drama. Comedy is drama exaggerated, heightened, and enriched. The legend is that, on his deathbed, Noel Coward was asked if dying was hard. "No, dying is easy," he reportedly replied, "Comedy is hard."

I'm convinced that the training of new animators is made doubly difficult because so much of the stuff of animation is comedic, even farcical. The temptation is to begin acting training by analyzing what kind of movement is funny and why—as if the movement itself has inherent entertainment value. It is easy for the new animator to overlook the important correlation between comedy and drama. How many animators cut their teeth on an animated *Hamlet* or *Merchant of Venice* after all?

Comedy is not a stand-alone form. It is a spin-off of tragedy. Before comedy, there was tragedy. Comedy came about when we decided to make fun of how serious we are. Laughter is actually an evasion of despair. (Warning! I'm about to get philosophical again!) We're all staring into the jaws of death, and we spend most of our lives trying not to think about it. Hence, we laugh. Ultimately, the joke is on us because we die anyway. Comedy looks the awful truth directly in the face and shrugs. Or spits. Or stamps its foot.

Former *New York Times* drama critic Walter Kerr, in his marvelous and essential book, *Tragedy and Comedy* (now out of print, by the way), draws the line between comedy and drama by citing the ancient Greek tale of Oedipus, which is about a man who marries his own mother and kills his own father. When he realizes what he had done, he is so anguished that he puts out his own eyes and banishes himself into the desert. That's a tragedy. But if Oedipus, on his way out of town, passes another blind guy who has killed his own father and married his own mother, the situation becomes comedic. Why is that? Because we can't handle the idea of two Oedipuses! The awfulness and pain is too much to bear, and so we laugh. Walter Kerr wrote another wonderful book that, happily, is *not* out of print, entitled *The Silent Clowns*. It's all about Chaplin and Keaton and the gang, and is a must-read.

Playwright Neil Simon finds a dividing line between drama and comedy in a fight he had with his wife. They were living in New York on Central Park West, and they were having a fight while she was cooking dinner. He doesn't remember what the fight was about, but it doesn't matter. She was furious, so furious that when she took a package of frozen peas out of the freezer, she slammed it on the counter to emphasize her point. Just then, Simon recognized that what she was doing was drama. But, if she had taken that same package of peas and *thrown* it at him, it would have become comedy! At one level it is drama, but extended, heightened, it becomes comedy.

Charlie Chaplin, whose work I like to cite in my Acting for Animators classes, created the ultimate optimist with his Little Tramp. No matter how many lemons life dealt him, he would make lemonade. But his optimism and cleverness would not be funny if he wasn't being optimistic in the face of death. Watch how he makes fun of the rich, most notably in *Modern Times*. Money won't buy you a seat in heaven.

Woody Allen, to name a modern-day counterpoint to Chaplin, is the ultimate pessimist. He wakes up every morning and confronts the cold reality of his ultimate demise. And then he lives the day the best way he can. When a car splashes him with a mud puddle, Woody figures that comes with the turf. If his wife runs off with another man, that is only to be expected. If he falls in love with another man's wife, well, why would nature *not* put him through such anguish? That's life.

The comedy of both Chaplin and Allen depend on their maintaining their particular perspective on human mortality. Both men are funny to watch physically because their movement is informed by their psychology. Chaplin has that spring in his step, always heading out for a brighter day. Woody Allen has high anxiety, angst, knowing that no matter what he says or does, it's going to be curtains sooner than he wants.

To repeat: comedy is drama extended, heightened, enriched, and exaggerated. Any good comedy script, if acted slowly, will play as a drama. Neil Simon comedy will withstand this litmus test. Any good Disney comedy will play as a drama. Tragedy and comedy are bedmates. Charlie Chaplin was inspired by the infamous Donner party with its rumored cannibalism and starvation when he came up with his shoe-eating sequence in *Gold Rush*.

In his book *Chuck Amuck*, Chuck Jones says that "comedy is unusual people in real situations; farce is real people in unusual situations" (1989, 142). I would add that all people are unusual, and all people are us. A good comedy character, regardless of the vehicle, is one we can identify with. If he is too much of an oddball, we will distance ourselves from him.

Farce

Animation lends itself strongly to farce. When Wile E. Coyote tries to run through the cave entrance he painted on the side of the mountain, only to flatten himself against the rocks, that's farce. When Sylvester climbs up on the stool and finally gets access to Tweety's cage, only to discover a salivating bulldog where the bird ought to be, that's farce. When Bugs Bunny falls off the cliff, tumbles half a mile to the ground and is only punished with a spinning head, that's farce. When the Tasmanian Devil eats several sticks of dynamite, thinking they are a roast turkey, and the resulting stomach explosion causes only indigestion and surprise, that's farce.

Mack Sennett's silent films, particularly the Keystone Kops series, were farce, as were some of the films of Buster Keaton and Charlie Chaplin. When the Little Tramp gets caught in the spinning cogs of the giant factory machine in *Modern Times*, that's farce. In reality, a person would surely die if he got sucked into the innards of a giant machine but in farce, the characters rarely die. This is why animation is actually a better medium for comedy of this sort than live action is. In animation, you can crash cars harder, toss characters from greater heights, even have them get shot through with shotgun pellets—and still survive.

Another element of farce is that machines and mechanical devices are the enemy. Guns are likely to explode in the character's face, elevators are likely to go down when they should go up, airplanes will run out of gas at the most inopportune moment, the electric razor will go nuts and shave a path across the top of the character's head. Farce is about mechanics, mechanical things gone wrong, timing, and the surprise element. Farce is definitely not the place to be worrying much about a lot of in-depth character analysis. Typically, characters in farce are pretty one-dimensional. Wile E. Coyote doesn't need any deeper character analysis. He's living in the desert, he's hungry, and fast food is nearby—a tasty Road Runner. Chaplin's character in *Modern Times* is just a workaday kind of guy, happy to have a gig, a full tummy, and a warm bed. When he gets accidentally swept up in labor protests, he doesn't even realize what is happening because he is completely uninformed about politics.

Though farce has been with us since caveman days, it is only now fully coming into its own. For an overview of the form, read Albert Bermel's marvelous history, *Farce: The Comprehensive and Definitive Account of One of the World's Funniest Art Forms* (1982).

Caricature

You can hold a mirror up to everything in nature, in which case you have a photograph. Or you can hold a mirror up only to quirks, in which case you have caricature. Caricature, in a way, holds an imperfect mirror up to nature, emphasizing those aspects of reality that you, the artist, consider most important.

Annibale Carracci (1560–1609), a naturalistic draughtsman of the Bolognese School, was the world's first caricaturist. He explained his art this way: "Is not the caricaturist's task exactly the same as the classical artist's? Both see the lasting truth behind the surface of mere outward appearance. Both try to help nature accomplish its plan. The one may strive to visualize the perfect form and to realize it in his work, the other to grasp the perfect deformity, and thus reveal the very essence of a personality. A good caricature, like every work of art, is more true to life than reality itself" (Lambourne 1983, 7).

The important thing to realize about caricature is that, before you can caricature a character, you must first have a clear understanding of what the character is really like. It's that thing about comedy being drama extended. First ask what's true. Then enhance it.

The Medium
10

Storytelling Versus Computer Games

Disney-style animation is basic storytelling, the kind of thing that has been going on for over two thousand years in one form or another. Even before that, all the way back to the days when we were wearing loincloths and sitting around campfires, messengers would tell stories of distant wars they witnessed.

Storytelling, if it aims to evoke emotion in the audience, requires distance between the performers and the audience. The idea is to allow the audience to experience emotions, such as fear, with safety, in their seats. The actors and the audience are collaborators, pretending together, and the audience "suspends its disbelief" in the proceedings. In other words, the audience pretends it does not know that what is happening on stage is not real. Medea is not really killing her children. If the audience did not suspend its disbelief, someone would call the cops, yes?

Computer games are a different thing, in pursuit of a different kind of audience response. As soon as you invite the audience to play the part of a character in the play, the theatrical illusion is broken. The person playing the game knows it is a game, but that margin of safe distance is removed. The player will pull the trigger, jump out of the airplane, whatever. He causes the action to happen, is a participant. He no longer is just watching and relating, and the theatrical experience is very different.

I have heard animators talk about the day when storytelling and computer games will merge. Visionaries speak of "total immersion" games in which the player is part of a virtual other world, a place where the characters are more real than reality, more believable than your mama, more frightening than one of ILM's dinosaurs. No doubt we will see projects of this scope at some point down the road. Technology is a marvelous thing. But I don't think total immersion will ever take the place of regular storytelling. It's apples and oranges. One requires distance, the other doesn't.

Aristotle, in the *Poetics*, talks about "unity of action" in drama. The creator of a play starts with a Big Idea, a theme, and, in essence, works backward, creating characters and situations that will lead the audience ultimately to discover the Big Idea. All of the smaller actions within the story support the bigger "action" of the theme. The hipbone is connected to the thighbone. Action leads to action leads to action leads to action.

Do computer games have themes, morals? Maybe. As best as I can tell, they mostly are battles of wits and reflexes, whether we are skulking around in castles or running through the jungle. We're trying to avoid being eaten, shot, or disintegrated while we eat, shoot, and disintegrate the other guy. Well, okay, I can see where that could be fun and get your pulse rate up—but it is a very long way from the theatrical experience of *Death of a Salesman* or even *Snow White and the Seven Dwarfs*.

The acting lesson for game designers is this: The audience empathizes with and is moved by emotion in the characters. If you want your game to be a theatrical experience and not the cyber equivalent of Mister Toad's Wild Ride, you will have to start with a story that has a point, and you'll have to create characters with feelings, emotions. There's a new game on the market as I write this, called The Sims. I haven't played it yet, but I hear that the characters fall in love, get divorces, fight battles, and so on. If so, this could be a step toward total involvement with empathic response.

Television Commercials

The United States is the Big Kahuna of consumer societies. Americans sell things to one another, and television commercials are the main aortic valve to the sales monster. It is a misnomer to say that a television program is "sponsored by" this or that advertiser. Television shows exist in order to deliver good-humored consumers to the commercials, not the other way around. More correctly, the commercials are sponsored by the shows! Ever since the game show scandals in the 1950s, advertising on television programs has been sold magazine-style, and the contest among producers in Hollywood has been to see who can deliver the most valuable demographics as measured by age and spending habits. Presently, the most desirable television viewer is young, maybe 18–28 years old and female because she has plenty of money and is a fickle, style-conscious, impulse shopper. She'll go see the same movie ten times, will buy whatever CD is hot this month, and will make the fashion designer or clothing store exec-of-the-moment oil-sultan rich.

Though television commercials have always featured clever animation—Speedy Alka Seltzer, the Ajax elves, and Charlie the Star-Kist Tuna come immediately to mind—commercials today are absolutely lush with it. Computer animation has broadened production possibilities at the same time that the attention span of the average television viewer has contracted to an intake-breath duration. Quick-moving animation and quick-cutting editing tends to keep the viewer's finger off the channel selector. And since it isn't likely that consumers are going to develop longer attention spans any time soon, we can safely predict a booming future for animators who gravitate toward the world of television advertising. Here are a few tips for those of you itching to animate commercials.

1. Implied Visual Message

Television commercials are not about information. In fact, Consumer Reports did a study a few years ago and discovered that only one commercial in eighteen conveys any useful information at all. They're not about information; they're about emotion. The idea is to create a positive emotional association with the product. The implied visual message is "If I use this product, I will be like the person in the commercial" (i.e., "I will have a lovely family, plenty of sex and money, lots of laughs, and maybe a Pillsbury Dough Boy to play with!"). In the world of television advertising, nobody dies, nobody ever gets any diseases that can't be cured by a nonprescription drug, and all the kids are cute. Animated critters such as roaches, fleas, ticks, and flies die in commercials, but theirs is most often a farcical, going-down-in-flames kind of death.

2. No New Products

There really are no new products under the sun. When someone finally invents a cure for cancer, nobody will have to do any commercials for it. Cars are pretty much the same and they all fall apart at about 100,000 miles; pain relievers are pretty much the same; McDonald's and Burger King are pretty much the same. The strategy behind most commercials is to get the consumer to buy Product A instead of Product B, on the premise that she will buy something of that product genre anyway. (Over 60 percent of television advertising target the female consumer.) We want her to buy Tide instead of Ivory Snow, a Lexus instead of a Mercedes, Haagen-Dazs Ice Cream instead of Ben & Jerry's.

3. No Conflict

The situations in television commercials are not to be confused with those in movies or theatre. We have already talked about how a scene is a negotiation, but in commercials that is not always the case. Commercials have close to zero conflict. There are no real negatives in most commercials, no possibility of losing in a negotiation. It's a happy-go-lucky world. Remember the movie *The Truman Show?* Pretty much on target if you ask me.

4. Pictures, Not Words

One of the first things I teach actors who want to learn how to act in commercials is to start watching them with the sound turned off. The real power of television commercials is in the visuals. We're back again to the fact that our sense of sight is more powerful than our sense of hearing. This is the secret to political advertising. Doesn't matter what the politico is saying, just as long as he's kissing babies and standing in front of the American flag.

5. Playing to the Camera

In movies and television shows, it is unusual for the character, animated or otherwise, to speak directly to the camera. Mickey Mouse used to do it on the old Mickey Mouse Show, but you rarely see it. Speaking directly to the camera is known, in acting terms, as *breaking the fourth wall*. In other words, the standard relationship between the audience and the show on television is static. The viewer watches as the action unfolds but doesn't interact with the characters. If a character speaks directly into the camera, he is speaking directly on a one-to-one basis to each individual viewer who is watching the show on television. In other words, he pulls the viewer into the action, makes him an actor in the show.

There is a trick to speaking directly and dynamically to the camera: You—or your character—should talk to the camera as if it is a person who might talk back. A monologue is actually a duologue. If your character has to speak to the camera, you need to create the reaction of the person he is talking to. It is impossible to talk to "America." Even if forty million people are watching a commercial, they are forty million individual people, each of whom must think your character is talking directly to him.

When we talk to another person, we tend to watch that person's face to see if he is following us. That is because conversation is hierarchical in structure. We make a point and then, when that point is grasped, we can add more information on top of it, building steadily toward a final point. And when we watch the other person, our own face tends to animate. Eyebrows lift, eyes widen. For proof of this, set up your video camera and practice talking "at" it. Then talk "with" it, as if it is a person who might talk back.

This business of talking "with" rather than "at" is very important and bears reiterating. An animator has the temptation to make the character cute or cuddly. But if you want to really connect with your audience one-to-one, you need to make the facial expressions interactive.

I wrote a book for actors entitled *The Audition Book: Winning Strategies for Breaking into Theatre, Film, and TV*, which contains a lengthy chapter on the world of commercials. Many of the techniques used by live actors in commercials can be applied to animation, and I recommend you read the book.

Classroom Exercises II

Acting classes typically include group improvisations and theatre games, and my acting classes for animators are no exception. You will learn a lot—and in a more fundamental way—by getting up on your feet and playing games. The following have been kitchen-tested for animators. Each will help you understand some principle of acting.

Animal Exercises

Picture a watering hole in Africa on a hot day. The only water for miles around is in this hole. Animals that might normally be enemies put aside their instincts to fight and drink side by side. Now, all the animators in the room will pretend to be an animal. Pick one, and let's get started.

"What kind of animal would my character be if my character were an animal?" This is an excellent rehearsal technique, and you'd be surprised how it can stimulate you emotionally to take on animal qualities. Stanley Kowalski is a barely disguised ape. Observe his low power center, his animal awareness of the world around him, his preference for physical action rather than words. Same with Schwartzenegger's characters, for the most part, and Sylvester Stallone's Rocky. Alma, in Williams' play, *Summer and Smoke,* is a bird. So is the young woman in William Mastrosimone's *The Woolgatherer.*

For animators who may very well be animating an animal in the first place, the equation can work both ways. "What kind of a person would my animal be if my animal was a person?"

What Is My Profession?
What Is My Age?

Viola Spolin, the mother of the improv group Second City, wrote a marvelous book, called *Improvisation for the Theater*. It contains lots of theatre games and improvs designed to loosen up the actor's instrument. One of the games in the book is good for animators to learn, and I try to include it when I teach. Here's the setup: There's a bus stop, a bench. Everybody in the class picks a profession and, one by one, they go up and wait for the bus. The idea is to avoid showing the audience what profession has been chosen. Just wait for the bus. You would be amazed at how little you have to do in order to communicate a chosen profession to the audience. One day, I saw an animator go wait for the bus, sitting quietly, evidently lost in some lovely, rhythmic thought. "You're a composer, a musician," said someone in the class. The animator was shocked because that was precisely what she had chosen and she was doing virtually nothing but listening to music in her mind. Audiences are smart creatures. You don't have to hit them over the head. Now try the same exercise, selecting age instead of profession.

Given Circumstances Game

When you do something—say, enter a room, you know (1) where you are, (2) what is happening, and (3) why it is happening. Simple, right? You'd be surprised how a simple thing like this can trip up beginning actors and animators. The temptation is to do things in order to be amusing. Stick with concrete circumstances, and it will work better, trust me.

I like to get animators up and on their feet in this exercise. I give everybody the following script and then send them up on stage, two at a time. (On the CD-ROM that accompanies this book, you'll find this exercise performed three different times by two actors from my acting class in San Francisco.)

PERSON #1:	Good morning.
PERSON #2:	What's so good about it?
PERSON #1:	Did you sleep well last night?
PERSON #2:	You know damned well how I slept.
PERSON #1:	Is there anything for breakfast?

PERSON #2: Fix it yourself.

PERSON #1: Listen, I think we ought to talk about this.

PERSON #2: I think that's a very good idea.

The object of the exercise is to change the given circumstances. Person #1, for example, might enter the room in a great mood, happy as a lark because he just got word that he was accepted in grad school. Person #2 didn't sleep well last night because Person #1 was snoring. So Person #1 has no idea why Person #2 is in a sour mood and has to react to that. Or Person #1 may be operating on the presumption that it isn't morning at all, but afternoon. Maybe he's joking when he says "Good morning." And Person #2 has to play off the reality of whatever Person #1 brings into the room.

Suppose Person #1 had a bad night and Person #2 had a great night? Person #1 enters with a hangover, say, seeking some coffee. Person #2 is playful. Look at the script again. The lines belonging to Person #2 may, at first glance, seem confrontational. Not necessarily. They may very well be playful. Depends on the given circumstances. Maybe Person #2 was kept up all night by Person #1's amorous advances. It was a night like no other, one for the record books. Person #2 is energized; Person #1 is pooped. This game can go on for hours if the players are inventive. Person #1 just won the lottery; Person #2 is pregnant. Person #1 has decided to move to Paris; Person #2 gambled away the family savings last night. And on and on and on . . .

Gibberish

One student gives a lecture or demonstrates a product, in gibberish, while another student "interprets" for him. Pretend it is a speech at the United Nations. The speaker's language is intelligible, without interpretation. The value in this exercise is that it teaches the importance of intention and highlights the relatively less important value of the words themselves.

Opera

The game can be played improvisationally or with memorized lines from a script. Sing everything, the fuller and bigger, the better. This game is really fun for animators who have trouble getting up on stage.

Status Transaction Game

Two people go to opposite sides of the stage, facing each other. One pretends to be "the King" or "the Queen," and the other pretends to be "the slave." They pass one another in the palace hallway and exchange greetings. Those who are on the sidelines watching will note that the slave tends to bend forward, sending his power into the ground. He will also tend to give the monarch a wide berth when they pass, careful not to intrude on his space.

Boss and Workers Game

Three people are involved. Set up three chairs on stage, side-by-side. The boss sits in the middle chair, and two workers sit in chairs on either side. When the boss talks to the worker on his right, the worker on his left makes faces at him. When he talks to the worker on his left, the worker on the right makes faces at him. If the boss catches one of the workers making a face at him, he "fires" him. The fired worker goes back to the audience, and is replaced by another worker.

The interesting thing about this super-fun game is that it works best when the worker who is making faces really exaggerates things. If he stands on his chair, waves perspiration odor at the boss, that kind of thing. It is hysterically funny to watch the offending worker try to act casual when he has been almost caught in the act of making faces.

I am fond of reminding my too-serious acting students that acting is supposed to be fun! "That's why they call them plays!" (Ed Hooks, 1944–). Yet, even some of the most talented animators balk when it comes time to do improvs in my classes. I want to emphatically urge you to be a joiner next time you're invited to play the games. Yes, it is silly; yes, it is embarrassing at times. On the other hand, once you learn a lesson on your feet, you're not likely to forget it!

The Iron Giant

An Acting Analysis

12

The *Iron Giant*, directed by Brad Bird, is a magnificent achievement in American animation. I had nothing whatever to do with the production of this film and, as of this writing, have never even met Brad Bird, but I am so enthusiastic about its merits that I want every reader of this book to see it, to study it for the acting lessons it contains. To that end, I am providing the following acting analysis of a few scenes from the movie. There is no scientific basis for my selection, only personal inclination. When something jumped out at me, acting-wise, I wrote it down to share with you. The scenes are titled as you will find them in the published DVD, which is generally available for purchase or rental.

The basic story involves complications that arise when a friendly, meat-eating, fifty-foot tall, iron giant crash-lands on earth and is befriended by a ten-year-old boy. The U.S. government—in the person of Kent Mansley—believes the creature is a front for some kind of communist plot and tries to destroy the Giant. The boy, Hogarth Hughes, with the help of a local artist and junk dealer, hides his new friend. During the course of the movie, the Giant learns what it means to be human, as Hogarth learns what it means to be an adult. Everybody learns what it means to have a dream. In the end, the Giant is the best friend this earth has ever had, and he willingly sacrifices to save the planet. (That's all I'll say about the end of the story, in case you haven't seen it.)

Before examining the scenes, keep in mind a couple of overall notes. First, I told you about the value of adrenaline moments, remember? In *The Iron Giant*, scene after scene is an adrenaline moment. The way to judge whether a scene fits the criteria is to ask if it is likely that the characters in the scene will remember the scene when they are in their old age. "Oh yeah, that was the day I met your mom, Hogarth. That damned squirrel climbed up my pants leg, and we had havoc in that diner. Heh, heh . . ."

Second, I have repeatedly spoken of the importance of establishing a sense of empathy, which *The Iron Giant* does in spades, and I have attempted to point out some of the techniques that were used to create that reaction. Now, to the scenes.

Scene 2: "Squirrelly at the Diner"

Hogarth Hughes has captured a squirrel and wants to keep it as a pet. As the scene begins, he is pedaling his bicycle through the seaside town of Rockwell (as in Norman Rockwell, perhaps?), Maine, with his squirrel, in transit to his mother's place of employment, the local diner.

ACTING NOTE #1—The dockworkers are minor players, extras in the scene, but notice that each of them is engaged in specific chores. Each is pursuing an objective. One fellow is moving boxes, another is coiling rope, and two others are collaborating on opening a container.

ACTING NOTE #2—As Hogarth enters the diner, he passes a man wearing a hat, sitting at the counter, reading a newspaper. Notice that the man mouths the words as he reads. Excellent character observation. Haven't we all seen people do that?

ACTING NOTE #3—Hogarth meets Dean for the first time, telling him that the squirrel has escaped and has run under his table. Significantly, the first time we—the audience—see Dean, he is asleep, still holding the newspaper, with its bold headlines about the Russian satellite, in his hands. This conveys a lot of information. First, Dean is following current events. He's literate. Second, he's a "night person," in contrast to everybody else in the diner. It is likely that he is eating breakfast after working all night. Note his day-old beard. And the sunglasses suggest that he's not a fan of bright light. His clothing is black, in contrast to the typical earth tones worn by everybody else. He's a nonconformist.

ACTING NOTE #4—The squirrel crawls up Dean's pants leg just as Hogarth's mother, Annie, approaches the table. Note how Dean at first successfully hides the discomfort of the squirrel in his pants, trying to be a good friend to Hogarth. The rule of acting is "play an action until something happens to make you play a different action." The squirrel going up the pants leg is the motivation for a new action. What Dean does about it is to "cover," to try to downplay the tickling going on down there. Following the same acting principle, the squirrel finally reaches Dean's crotch level, motivating him to stand up, unzip his pants, and release havoc into the diner.

Scene 4: "An Iron Giant"

The Iron Giant tries to eat the local power station, and Hogarth saves his life.

ACTING NOTE #1—The first time we see the Giant, he is searching for food. He's hungry. This is a point of empathy because humans act to survive. We all have to eat. So, immediately, we can identify with a primal need in the creature.

Scene 7: "Something Big"

We meet Kent Mansley from the U.S. government for the first time. Note that his power center is in his chin.

ACTING NOTE #1—After Mansley sees the ruins of the power tower and scoffs at the suggestion that a "giant monster" may be responsible, he is asked which part of the U.S. government he represents. Immediately after the editing cut from the close-up of Mansley to a long shot of him and Marvin the worker, he assumes a performance mode. Notice how he rocks first back on his feet and then struts forward, putting on a show for Marvin, trying to intimidate and impress him. That backward rocking is different from the way other characters begin their walks, and it suggests a person who likes to be on stage, who is full of himself.

ACTING NOTE #2—Mansley turns into a coward when he discovers the monster has eaten half of his car. Note how his rhythm and power center shift. When he drags Marvin out of the woods to see the car, notice how he is leaning forward, power going into the ground, low status to Marvin, who now seems to be the Rock of Gibraltar. Notice how his arms begin to wildly gesticulate. The "performance" he was doing for Marvin only moments before is totally eradicated, the mask has fallen, and the "real" Kent Mansley stands before us. Brilliant.

Scene 8: "The Luckiest Kid"

Hogarth gets to know his new friend.

ACTING NOTE #1—Here is where we first start feeling real empathy for the Giant. Note that in his first appearance in the scene, he is very robotlike, stomping toward Hogarth in a manner that could well mean doom for the boy. When they finally come face-to-face, the interaction begins. The Giant, with great effort, imitates the sitting posture of the boy. Clearly, sitting in this way is not a normal movement for the Giant. He sort of collapses onto the ground. He's trying to be friendly, and we empathize.

ACTING NOTE #2—After the Giant gives Hogarth the power station shut-off switch, in gratitude for Hogarth's having saved his life, we get a close-up of the Giant's head. Note the way he tilts his head to the left, almost puppylike. Again, we relate to his efforts to be friendly. The tilt of the head expresses curiosity and an eagerness to learn.

ACTING NOTE #3—When the Giant makes a first effort to speak, saying "Blah, blah, blah," he rocks his head back and forth. Talking is fun! Like a game of "fetch"! We can relate. The important thing is in the rocking of the head.

ACTING NOTE #4—After the Giant distinguishes between a rock and a tree, Hogarth gets excited about being "the luckiest kid in America." Note the Giant's physical reaction to Hogarth's obvious delight. The Giant doesn't know what everybody is so happy about, but he's happy to be happy, too!

Scene 9: "Train Coming"

ACTING NOTE #1—The Giant starts dozing off when Hogarth is so long-winded. Another point of empathy. The Giant needs not only to eat, but also to sleep, in order to survive. We can relate. Perhaps as important is that the Giant is already learning good manners. Rather than go to sleep, which he could easily do, he wakes himself back up so he can continue to be a good audience for Hogarth. Who among us has not done that at the most boring parties in the world? More empathy.

ACTING NOTE #2—After the Giant tries to eat the railroad track, the crossing signal begins to ring and blink the red light. It happens quickly, but note the Giant's reaction. He drops the track from his mouth and switches his playful attention to the crossing signal. A new toy! More empathy. The Giant is an overgrown cross between a child and a puppy, it seems.

ACTING NOTE #3—The Giant puts the broken train track back together again. Rather than simply have him do the chore, the animators went for the playful game approach. The Giant is eager to do his master's bidding, to please Hogarth. He wants to get the tracks back together just right, and so he frets over it until it is too late, and he is hit by the train. This is an important moment in the story. Later, we learn that the Giant has a true talent for arts and crafts. Again, we can relate to the idea of perfectionism.

Scene 11: "Hands-On"

ACTING NOTE #1—Hogarth's blessing of dinner is a marvelous forty-five seconds of animation, thanks to animation supervisor Tony Fucile. Acting-wise, the thing that makes it interesting is that he has to play two actions at once: (1) protecting the Giant's hand from being discovered and (2) saying grace. In terms of priority, it is more important for Hogarth—as it would be for any child—to protect the Giant's hand. And so, saying grace becomes an action in pursuit of a double objective. The swinging pendulum of the grandfather clock on the wall near the dinner table is important, too. The steady tick-tock rhythm of the pendulum contrasts with, and highlights, Hogarth's inner rhythm, which is near panic.

ACTING NOTE #2—Kent Mansley leers at Hogarth's mother in a frankly sexual way. Hogarth notices this, setting up the competition between the boy and the government agent. It's primal. Hogarth is the "man of the house" now that his father is dead, even if his functions do not manifest themselves in a sexual way. Mansley is, from the first instance, an interloper. Later on, we will see Mansley sitting in Hogarth's father's favorite easy chair and in his place at the breakfast table. This is very smart storytelling, because the competition between Hogarth and Mansley function on multiple levels, one of them primal.

Scene 15: "We Like Dean"

ACTING NOTE #1—The Giant eats a car, and the car horn goes off. Under pressure to silence it, he goes through a decision-making process. There are a couple of acting notes in this moment. (1) Emotion leads to action. (Thinking leads to conclusions.) Because the Giant must silence the alarm quickly, the solution springs from emotion.

(2) When a character is indecisive, it is best to have him go from specific action to specific action in his thinking. Note how the Giant considers various options for silencing the alarm. He looks to his right ("Is there something over there I can use to silence it? No.") He looks to his left. ("Is there something over there, then? No.") He looks down, getting the idea to sit on the car. It is a one-two-three-step mental process, very specific. (This also creates greater identification by the audience, who are thinking, emotional humans.) When sitting on the car doesn't work, the Giant tries to silence it by hammering on it. (I actually did that once with a car alarm. Didn't work for me, either.) Finally, he figures out the best solution, one which uses his super strength. He throws the car several miles out into the ocean.

ACTING NOTE #2—Hogarth's case of the coffee jitters is an excellent sequence. The acting note has to do with the effect of external substances—in this case, caffeine. The animator allowed the substance to have the physical effect (nervousness, quicker rhythms, racing mind) on Hogarth, and then he acted to control it. As wired as Hogarth is, he is not grasping at his heart or getting afraid. Instead, he tries to behave with Dean as if this is perfectly normal. Dean sees right through it, of course. Another nice thing about this sequence is that Hogarth learns a lesson in life ("too much coffee will make you nervous") from Dean, who becomes a true father figure later in the story.

Scene 16: "Fast Friends"

ACTING NOTE #1—Mansley's manic side surfaces in the soda fountain. Note how his body rhythm changes and the arms gesticulate. It's become a pattern that we can recognize, and from which we can draw conclusions about Mansley's strengths and weaknesses. Anxiety is a high power center. See how the arms are flailing around the head? Also, note that Mansley is stooped over when he goes into his Sputnik tirade. Logically, the stoop is motivated by his desire to get eye-to-eye with Hogarth but, in a status transaction—which is the acting lesson—that kind of stoop comes across as low-status, unpowerful. Mansley's manic quality is his Achilles' heel.

Scene 20: "Soulful Under the Stars"

ACTING NOTE #1—The scene with the deer in the woods strikes all kinds of emotional chords, of course—Bambi and ET most notably. How delighted the Giant is when he gets his first good look at the pretty deer! A new playmate! More empathy. The gently offered finger of friendship, followed by a gunshot.

ACTING NOTE #2—The Giant is depressed and, as he lies in the junkyard that night, notice how physically heavy he is, how much effort it takes to move a finger. Gravity is almost too much to overcome. Death equates to gravity. That's probably why they call them "graves."

Scene 23: "Weapons to Bear"

ACTING NOTE #1—After the Giant almost kills Hogarth, Dean accuses him of being a "big gun." The Giant says, "I am not a gun." Note how his palms are facing up, submissively. His body language says, "I won't hurt you."

Scene 24: "I Am Not a Gun"

ACTING NOTE #1—The Giant saves the two boys who fall off a building in town, much to the gratitude of the townsfolk. When Hogarth and Dean arrive on the scene, the Giant picks up Hogarth and once again says, "I am not a gun." This time his body language expresses confidence, assurance. No turned-out palms. The Giant has chosen what he wants to be, and he is decidedly not a gun. The energy has returned to his body; he has overcome gravity and death.

Scene 26: "Arsenals Unleashed"

The Giant's transformation from grieving friend, when he believes that Hogarth has been killed, to fighting machine is accomplished by removing all of the vestiges of humanity that have been carefully layered on his character. As a weapon, he is thoughtlessly, automatically, knee-jerk reactive to assault. No compassion, no emotion, just killing. The Giant's movements lose their grace. Now he moves like a recoiling rifle.

Scene 28: "The Giant's Choice"

ACTING NOTE #1—As before, when the Giant tried to decide how to silence the car horn, he now goes through another, far more complex decision-making process. Still, acting-wise, the thoughts are specific. When Hogarth tells him that, when the missile comes back to earth, "we will all die," the Giant stands erect and gazes at the townspeople gathered together like so many deer in the woods. The Giant looks upward, his gaze following the trajectory of the missile. The decision is made. When he crouches to tell Hogarth goodbye, he has become more human than any of us—gentle and caring. He makes a joke, cheering up Hogarth. "Me go. You stay. No following."

When I set out to write this book, I had no way of knowing that my work would be enlightened by this great movie. *The Iron Giant* is excellent and, in my opinion, merits its own course number in animation schools. (And, actually, the devil in me says it would be fun to compare and contrast it with DreamWorks' *Road to El Dorado*.) I cannot find a false moment in *Iron Giant*, not a frame I would change. It is a case study in good acting and it is inspired storytelling animation. Buy it and study it. Then show it to your kids. And whisper a little thanks to Brad Bird while you're at it.

Postscript

What Is Method Acting?

Method acting is, to many people, acting itself. They may not know how it works or where it came from, but they have heard somewhere that it leads to truthfulness on stage and that our greatest actors are Method trained. It has unfortunately been promoted as a synoym of acting excellence, and that simply isn't true.

Sharon M. Carnicke, associate professor as well as associate dean of theatre at the University of Southern California, has done us all a great favor by writing *Stanislavsky in Focus*, which everyone should read. The primary value in Carnicke's book is that it draws a firm line between Stanislavsky's "System" and Lee Strasberg's "Method." That alone is worth the price.

It amazes me that Method ating is so often recommended to animators because I don't see where it is all that useful. Mainly, Strasberg's Method is about internal triggers rather than physical action. Method acting classes tend to feature plenty of tears and hair tearing. I would be happier seeing animators reading Michal Chekhove over Lee Strasberg.

Read Carnicke for an in-depth study of this subject. For now, I will share with you a brief overview of Strasberg's Method as it relates to Stanislavsky's System.

The favored acting style of the mid-nineteenth century essentially amounted to posturing. Actors did not try to experience real emotion on stage, but to show the audience how it would look if they did experience real emotion. You've seen the drawings and photographs of those old-school actors. Actresses in swoon postures, actors displaying mock anger, silly-looking stuff. There were books written, in fact, with drawings of the various poses and emotions that actors were supposed to imitate.

Then came Konstantin Stanislavsky, who got mightily impressed with research being done by Sigmund Freud and Pavlov. Those men were mapping the human emotions, getting into things like conditioned response. Pavlov did his famous experiment with the dog and the bell, ringing the bell whenever he fed the dog. After a while, he only had to ring the bell and the dog's mouth would water. Stanislavsky was fascinated and figured actors ought to be able to use these new ideas. Why couldn't actors ring a bell and have their mouths water? Why must actors pretend to have emotion on stage when they might experience the real McCoy?

And so, on June 23, 1897, Stanislavsky met in a Moscow restaurant with producer/director Nemerovich Denchenko to discuss the formation of a new theatre and acting school that would apply this new thinking about psychology.

The main focus of Stanislavsky's early work with his actors at the new Moscow Arts Theatre was the search for emotional "triggers"—memories, smells, sights—whatever would stimulate true emotion in the actor. The actors applied their new skills to productions of plays by a new playwright, Anton Chekhov. And the rest, as they say . . .

When the Moscow Art Theatre performed in New York in 1922, American actors picked up the Stanislavsky approach. In particular, Lee Strasberg adopted and expanded on Stanislavsky's ideas. He and a few other very serious theatre folk formed the Group Theatre in New York, and Strasberg conducted regular acting classes for the resident company of actors. Later, after the dissolution of the Group Theatre, Strasberg headed up the Actor's Studio, from whence sprang Marlon Brando, James Dean, Paul Newman, Al Pacino, and a host of other actors whose names we all know.

Most actors today have been trained in the principles first laid down by Stanislavsky, though there are variations, and many have been taught in methods that are offshoots of Strasberg's work. Some teachers put emphasis on the development of the imagination, others put emphasis on the search for emotional triggers. But, one way or another, it all goes back to Pavlov's dog. Actors are always trying to get their mouths to water on cue.

Recommended Reading and Other Resources

Recommended Reading

There are thousands of acting books in print and at least dozens at any halfway decent bookstore. You probably won't hurt yourself by reading any of them. Terms may vary from text to text—*emotional recall* in one book will be known as *affective memory* in the next, that kind of thing—but it is pretty much all in pursuit of naturalistic, psychologically truthful performance. If you were to get hold of something experimental, like say Brecht or Grotowski, you'll know it right away.

My short reading list would include

On the Technique of Acting by Michael Chekhov

On Acting by Sanford Meisner

Respect for Acting and *A Challenge for the Actor* by Uta Hagen

Stanislavsky in Focus by Sharon M. Carnicke

Strasberg at the Actors Studio, edited by Robert H. Hethmon

Impro by Keith Johnstone

Acting: The First Six Lessons by Richard Boleslavsky

Laban for Actors and Dancers by Jean Newlove

Preparing a Character and *An Actor Prepares* by Konstantin Stanislavsky

Laban Movement Schools

Jean Newlove Centre for Laban Studies
Flat 1, 44 Woodville Gardens
London W52LQ
Fax: +44 (0) 181 997 3007
E-mail: jean@newlovemakepeace.demon.co.uk

Laban/Bartenieff Institute of Movement Studies
234 Fifth Ave., Room 203
New York, NY 10001
(212) 477-4299

Leslie Bishko
Vancouver Institute of Media Arts
837 Beatty Street, 2d floor
Vancouver, BC Canada V6B 2M6
(604) 682-2787

Laban Movement Books

Your Move: A New Approach to the Study of Movement and Dance by Ann Hutchinson Guest (Gordon and Breach, 1983)

Laban for Actors and Dancers by Jean Newlove (Routledge, 1993)

The Mastery of Movement (2d ed.) by Rudolf Laban, revised by Lisa Ullmann (Macdonald and Evans, Ltd., 1960)

Choreutics by Rudolf Laban, edited by Lisa Ullmann (Macdonald and Evans, Ltd., 1966)

Body Movement: Coping with the Environment by Imgard Bartenieff (Gordon Breach Science Publishers, 1980)

Phrasing and Effort: Significant Components of Dance Dynamics by Vera Maletic (Ohio State University, 1984)

Works Cited

Bermel, Albert. 1982. *Farce: The Comprehensive and Definitive Account of One of the World's Funniest Art Forms.* New York: Touchstone/Simon & Schuster.

Bishko, Leslie. 1999. Conversation with author about Laban Movement Theory, October.

Blair, Preston. 1990. *How to Animate Film Cartoons.* Laguna Hills, CA: Walter Foster Publishing.

Blum, Deborah. 1998. "Face It." *Psychology Today* (Sept./Oct.): 32.

Brook, Peter. 1987. *The Shifting Point.* New York: Theatre Communications Group.

————. 1995. *The Open Door: Thoughts on Acting and Theatre.* New York: Theatre Communications Group.

Carnicke, Sharon M. 1998. *Stanislavsky in Focus.* Newark, NJ: Harwood Academic Publishers.

Chekhov, Michael. 1991. *On the Technique of Acting.* New York: HarperCollins.

Culhane, Shamus. 1990. *Animation from Script to Screen.* New York: St. Martin's Press.

————. 1998. *Talking Animals and Other People.* New York: Da Capo.

Darwin, Charles. 1991. *The Expression of the Emotions in Man and Animals.* 3d ed. Edited by Paul Ekman. New York: Oxford University Press.

Diderot, Denis. 2000. "The Paradox of Acting." In *Theatre Theory Theatre: The Major Critical Texts,* edited by Daniel Gerould. New York: Applause Books.

Eisenstein, Sergie. 1942. *The Film Sense.* New York: Harcourt Brace Jovanovich.

Ekman, Paul, and Wallace Friesen. 1975. *Unmasking the Face.* Upper Saddle River, NJ: Prentice-Hall.

Ekman, Paul, R. W. Levenson, and W. V. Friesen. 1983. "Autonomic Nervous System Activity Distinguishes Between Emotions." *Science* 221: 1208–10.

Ekman, Paul, and O'Sullivan. 1991. "Facial Expression: Methods, Means, and Moues." In *Fundamentals of Nonverbal Behavior*, edited by R. S. Feldman and B. Rime. New York: Cambridge University Press.

Gallwey, W. Timothy. 1974. *The Inner Game of Tennis*. New York: Random House.

Hall, Edward T. 1969. *The Hidden Dimension*. New York: Doubleday.

Hodge, Allison, ed. 2000. *Twentieth-Century Actor Training*. New York: Routledge.

Hooks, Ed. 1996. *The Audition Book: Winning Strategies for Breaking into Theatre, Film, and Television*. New York: Backstage Books.

Hopcke, Robert H. 1989. *A Guided Tour of the Collected Works of C. G. Jung*. Boston: Shambhala.

Johnstone, Keith. 1979. *Impro: Improvisation and the Theatre*. New York: Routledge.

Jones, Chuck. 1989. *Chuck Amuck*. New York: Farrar, Straus & Giroux.

Kazan, Elia. 1988. *A Life*. New York: Alfred A. Knopf.

Kerr, Walter. 1975. *The Silent Clowns*. New York: Alfred A. Knopf.

Lambourne, Lionel. 1983. *Caricature*. London: Her Majesty's Stationery Office.

Maletic, Vera. 1984. *Phrasing and Effort: Significant Components of Dance Dynamics*. Columbus: Ohio State University Press.

Menache, Alberto. 2000. *Understanding Motion Capture for Computer Animation and Video Games*. San Francisco: Morgan Kaufmann.

Merritt, Russell, and J. B. Kaufman. 2000. *Walt in Wonderland: The Silent Films of Walt Disney*. Baltimore: Johns Hopkins University Press.

Minow, Newton, and Craig Lamay. 1996. *Abandoned in the Wasteland*. New York: Hill & Wang.

Robinson, David. 1985. *Chaplin: His Life and Art*. New York: McGraw-Hill.

Russell, James A., and Jose Miguel Fernandez-Dols. 1997. *The Psychology of Facial Expression*. New York: Cambridge University Press.

Spolin, Viola. 1999. *Improvisation for the Theatre: A Handbook of Teaching and Directing Techniques*. 3d ed. Evanston, IL: Northwestern University Press.

Sweet, Jeffrey. 1993. *The Dramatist's Toolkit: The Craft of the Working Playwright*. Portsmouth, NH: Heinemann.

Thomas, Frank, and Ollie Johnston. 1981. *The Illusion of Life: Disney Animation*. New York: Hyperion.

———. 1993. *The Disney Villain*. New York: Hyperion.

Wright, Robert. 1994. *The Moral Animal*. New York: Pantheon.

Young, Jeff. 1999. *Kazan: The Master Director Discusses His Films*. New York: Newmarket Press.

About the CD

This CD contains video clips illustrating seven essential acting concepts that are discussed in the book, as well as the various "efforts" (how an actor moves through space) delineated by Rudolf Laban. It is designed to offer actual demonstrations of the principles addressed in the book. In addition, on screen text helps guide you through the demonstrations and further expand upon the principles involved.

To use the CD, simply insert it into the CD-ROM drive on your computer. The CD should launch automatically and allow you to navigate through the improvisations and the demonstrations.

Systems Requirements:

Windows/PC

Pentium Processor (233 Mhz or higher)

Windows 95 (or higher)

64 MB RAM (more recommended)

SVGA Color Display (or better)

8x CD-ROM Drive (or faster)

Macintosh

PowerPC Processor

System 8 (or higher)

64 MB RAM (more recommended)

SVGA Color Display (or better)

8x CD-ROM Drive (or faster)